ECCENTRICS

21 Stories of Unusual and Remarkable People—With Exercises for Developing Critical Reading Skills

Henry Billings
Melissa Billings

 Jamestown Publishers

ECCENTRICS
21 Stories of Unusual and Remarkable People—With
Exercises for Developing Critical Reading Skills

Catalog No. 765

©1987 by Jamestown Publishers

Cover and Text Design by Deborah Hulsey Christie

Printed in the United States of America

  6 7 8 9 HS 98 97 96 95

ISBN 0-89061-464-4

Contents

GROUP THREE

To the Teacher

INTRODUCTION

> If a man does not keep pace with his companions, perhaps
> it is because he hears a different drummer. Let him step to
> the music which he hears, however measured or far away.
>
> Henry David Thoreau
> *Walden*

There have always been people who have stepped to the beat of a
different drummer, capturing the interest and imaginations of
those around them (and sometimes causing the more traditional
folks to gasp, shake their heads in amazement, or laugh
uproariously). The stories in *Eccentrics* are profiles of people
who lived their lives differently from most people. They range
from the lovable and the impressive to the bizarre. In some
stories it may be hard to draw the line between genius and
madness, eccentricity and insanity.

Eccentrics provides subject matter for thoughtful interpretation
and discussion, while challenging your students in four critical
reading categories: main idea, important details, inferences, and
vocabulary in context. *Eccentrics* can also help your students
to improve their reading rates. Timing of the selections is
optional, but many teachers find it an effective motivating
device.

Eccentrics consists of twenty-one units divided into three
groups of seven units each. All the stories in a group are on
the same reading level. Group One is at the sixth-grade reading
level, Group Two at the seventh, and Group Three at the eighth,
as assessed by the Fry Formula for Estimating Readability.

HOW TO USE THIS BOOK

Introducing the Book. This text, used creatively, can be an effective tool for learning certain critical reading skills. We suggest that you begin by introducing the students to the contents and format of the book. Examine the book with the students to see how it is set up and what it is about. Discuss the title. What is an eccentric? (An eccentric is a person with characteristics that most other people consider strange or off-beat. The key point is that eccentrics do not *try* to be different from those around them—they usually do not think of themselves as being odd. But if their behavior or beliefs are far enough removed from ordinary behavior or beliefs, they will be labeled eccentric by others. There are, of course, degrees of eccentricity. Some people are just a little weird; others are very weird indeed.) Read through the table of contents as a class, to gain an overview of the eccentrics who will be encountered.

The Sample Unit. To learn what is contained in each unit and how to proceed through a unit, turn to the Sample Unit on pages 10–15. After you have examined these pages yourself, work through the Sample Unit with your students, so that they may have a clear understanding of the purpose of the book and of how they are to use it.

The Sample Unit is set up exactly as the regular units are. At the beginning there is a photograph or illustration accompanied by a brief introduction to the story. The story is next, followed by four types of comprehension exercises: Finding the Main Idea, Recalling Facts, Making Inferences, and Using Words Precisely.

Begin by having someone in the class read aloud the introduction that appears with the picture. Then give the students a few moments to study the picture. Ask for their thoughts on what the story will be about. Continue the discussion for a minute or so. Then have the students read the story. (You may wish to time the students' reading, in order to help them improve their reading speed as well as their comprehension. A Words per Minute table is located in the back of the book, to help the students figure their reading rates.)

Then go through the sample questions as a class. An explanation of the comprehension skill and directions for answering the questions are given at the beginning of each exercise. Make sure all the students understand how to answer the four different types of questions and how to figure their scores. The correct answers and sample scores are filled in. Also, explanations of all the correct answers are given within the sample Main Idea and Making Inferences exercises, to help the students understand how to think through these question types.

As the students are working their way through the Sample Unit, be sure to have them turn to the Words per Minute table on pages 154 and 155 (if you have timed their reading) and the Reading Speed and Critical Reading Scores graphs on pages 156 and 157 at the appropriate points. Explain to the students the purpose of each, and read the directions with them. Be sure they understand how the table and graphs will be used. You will probably have to help them find and mark their scores for the first unit or two.

Timing the Story. If you are going to time your students' reading, explain to them your reason for doing so: to help them keep track of and improve their reading rates.

Here's one way of timing. Have all the students in the class begin reading the story at the same time. After one minute has passed, write on the chalkboard the time that has elapsed, and begin updating it at ten-second intervals (1:00, 1:10, 1:20, etc.). Tell the students to copy down the last time shown on the chalkboard when they have finished reading. They should write their reading time in the space designated after the story.

Have the students check their reading rates by using the Words per Minute table on pages 154 and 155. They should then enter their reading speed on the Reading Speed graph on page 156. Graphing their reading rates allows the students to keep track of improvement in their reading speed.

Working Through Each Unit. If the students have carefully completed all parts of the Sample Unit, they should be ready to tackle the regular units. In each unit, begin by having someone in the class read aloud the introduction to the story, just as you did in the Sample Unit. Discuss the topic of the story, and allow the students time to study the illustration.

Then have the students read the story. If you are timing them, have the students enter their reading time, find their reading speed, and record their speed on the graph after they have finished reading the story.

Next, direct the students to complete the four comprehension exercises *without* looking back at the story. When they have finished, go over the questions and answers with them. The students will grade their own answers and make the necessary corrections. They should then enter their Critical Reading Scores on the graph on page 157.

The Graphs. Students enjoy graphing their work. Graphs show, in a concrete and easily understandable way, how a student is progressing. Seeing a line of progressively rising scores gives students the incentive to continue to strive for improvement.

Check the graphs regularly. This will allow you to establish a routine for reviewing each student's progress. Discuss with each student what the graphs show and what kind of progress you expect. Establish guidelines and warning signals so that students will know when to approach you for counseling and advice.

RELATED TEXTS

If you find that your students enjoy and benefit from the stories and skills exercises in *Eccentrics,* you may be interested in *Aliens and UFOs, Heroes, Disasters!, Phenomena, Monsters, Calamities,* and *Apparitions,* seven related Jamestown texts. All feature high-interest stories and work in four critical reading comprehension skills. As in *Eccentrics,* the units in those books are divided into three groups, at reading levels six, seven, and eight.

He called himself the "luckiest fool alive." Shown here at the high point of his career, Shipwreck Kelly perches amid the towers and spires of New York City. His daring stunts brought him national fame and the cheers of thousands of fans. Kelly loved the popularity, but as with all good things, the glory couldn't last forever.

Alvin "Shipwreck" Kelly

He "just went up for a breath of fresh air." At least that is what he claimed. But Alvin "Shipwreck" Kelly's idea of getting a little fresh air was rather offbeat. On November 17, 1927, Kelly and his pilot took off from Curtiss Field, on Long Island, in a biplane. Hundreds of curious spectators gathered near the runway to see Shipwreck Kelly try another bizarre stunt. Earlier that year, Kelly had gained fame by spending twelve days and twelve hours sitting atop a flagpole on the roof of the St. Francis Hotel in Newark, New Jersey.

This time, however, the most famous flagpole sitter in the United States had something else in mind. He planned to sit on a ten-foot iron pole fastened to the top wing of a biplane. As the plane made its first pass over the airfield, Kelly climbed out of the cockpit. Gingerly, he pulled himself onto the top wing. Then he wrapped himself around the pole and waved to the crowd below. On the second pass over the airfield, Kelly wagged his foot over the edge of the wing. Then he climbed up the pole and sat on a small crossbar attached near the top. When the spectators saw him perched there on the third pass, they roared their approval. Shipwreck Kelly had pulled off another crowd-pleasing trick.

The 1920s were a fun-loving decade, filled with loony fads such as goldfish swallowing and marathon dancing. But the nuttiest craze of all was flagpole sitting. And the nuttiest flagpole sitter was Shipwreck Kelly. Kelly loved to court danger. He boasted that he had survived five sea disasters while serving in the navy in World War I. That earned him the nickname "Shipwreck." He also claimed to have walked away from two airplane crashes, three automobile accidents, and a train wreck—all without getting a scratch.

Kelly billed himself as the "luckiest fool alive." No one disputed the claim. He certainly was foolish. And he was lucky to live at a time when people would actually pay to watch him sit on a flagpole. Kelly sat on many flagpoles, but he preferred those on hotel rooftops. The hotels were grateful for the attention he attracted. They gave him free lodging, meals, and a cash advance. In addition, Kelly earned part of the fee that the hotel charged people to sit on the roof and watch the spectacle.

Shipwreck Kelly loved publicity. He also loved to smash old notions about the limits of human endurance. On June 21, 1930, Kelly climbed a 125-foot pole on the Steel Pier in Atlantic City. A disk about the size of a record album had been attached to the top. There Kelly made

himself as comfortable as possible. He was determined to break his own flagpole-sitting record of twenty-three days and seven hours. Kelly wanted to stay aloft for a full twenty-eight days. That, he felt, would be a record no rival flagpole sitter would ever break.

For the next twenty-eight days Kelly stayed on top of the pole. Thousands of people went by daily to witness the implausible stunt. They wondered how anyone could actually live on top of a flagpole day after day. But Kelly had all the details worked out. First of all, he devised a way to sleep without falling off. Before going to sleep, he would put his thumbs into small holes in the flagpole shaft. If he swayed while dozing, the twinge of pain in his thumbs caused him to right himself without waking. A hollow tube attached to the side of the pole served as his toilet. He even managed to bathe himself every now and then, with a sponge and a pail of water.

Shipwreck Kelly spent his time on the flagpole writing about his experience, listening to a radio, and reading his fan mail. He got about a hundred letters a day from admirers around the country. Kelly's wife and young child, Alvin, Jr., visited on Saturdays. They were hoisted up the pole in a special chair.

When Kelly finally reached his goal, everyone naturally expected him to come down. But Kelly must have been enjoying his life high above Atlantic City. He decided to stay put a little longer. A doctor checked him and pronounced him physically fit. Lack of exercise, however, was causing him to gain weight. To prevent any further weight gain, he cut back to just one meal a day.

At last, on the morning of August 9, Shipwreck Kelly let people know that he was coming down. He wanted to finish in style, so a barber was hoisted up to give him a haircut and a manicure. When Kelly finally descended the pole, twenty thousand screaming fans greeted him. It took him four minutes to slip down to the Steel Pier. When he hit the ground, he had trouble walking. After all, he hadn't taken a step since June 21. He had been aloft for 1,177 hours—more than forty-nine days. Shipwreck Kelly had broken his own record by more than six hundred hours.

The Steel Pier stunt was the highlight of Kelly's flagpole-sitting career. Kelly continued to sit on flagpoles around the country for another five years. But the glory days of flagpole sitting had passed. Such exhibitions of human endurance no longer fascinated people. Shipwreck Kelly slowly faded into obscurity. He collapsed and died on a New York sidewalk in 1952. Tucked under his arm was a scrapbook filled with old newspaper clippings about the exploits of Alvin "Shipwreck" Kelly. ∎

If you have been timed while reading this selection, enter your reading time below. Then turn to the Words per Minute table on page 154 and look up your reading speed (words per minute). When you are working through the regular units, you will then enter your reading speed on the graph on page 156.

READING TIME: Sample Unit

_____ : _____
Minutes   *Seconds*

How well did you read?

- *The four types of questions that follow appear in each unit in this book. The directions for each kind of question tell you how to mark your answers. In this Sample Unit, the answers are marked for you. Also, for the Main Idea and Making Inferences exercises, explanations of the answers are given, to help you understand how to think through these question types. Read through these exercises carefully.*

- *When you have finished all four exercises in a unit, you will check your work by using the answer key that starts on page 150. For each right answer, you will put a check mark (✓) on the line beside the box. For each wrong answer, you will write the correct answer on the line.*

- *For scoring each exercise, you will follow the directions below the questions. In this unit, sample scores are entered as examples.*

A FINDING THE MAIN IDEA

Look at the three statements below. One expresses the main idea of the story you just read. A good main idea statement answers two questions: it tells *who* or *what* is the subject of the story, and it answers the understood question *does what?* or *is what?* Another statement is *too broad*, it is vague and doesn't tell much about the topic of the story. The third statement is *too narrow*, it tells about only one part of the story.

Match the statements with the three answer choices below by writing the letter of each answer in the box in front of the statement it goes with.

M—Main Idea   B—Too Broad   N—Too Narrow

✓   N 1. To give the spectators a thrill, Shipwreck Kelly sat on a ten-foot iron pole fastened to the top wing of a biplane.
   [This statement is *too narrow*. It doesn't tell anything about Kelly's flagpole sitting.]

✓   B 2. During the 1920s, many entertainers tried unique stunts to gain attention and to make money.
   [This statement is *too broad*. While true, the statement doesn't tell us anything about Shipwreck Kelly.]

✓   M 3. Shipwreck Kelly, a determined publicity seeker, won national fame by setting flagpole-sitting records.
   [This statement is the *main idea*. It tells who Shipwreck Kelly was and what he did.]

__15__ Score 15 points for a correct *M* answer
__10__ Score 5 points for each correct *B* or *N* answer

__25__ TOTAL SCORE: Finding the Main Idea

B RECALLING FACTS

How well do you remember the facts in the story you just read? Put an x in the box in front of the correct answer to each of the multiple choice questions below.

1. One of the loony fads of the 1920s was
   - ☐ a. tree climbing.
   - ☑ b. goldfish swallowing. ✓
   - ☐ c. marathon road races.

2. Kelly earned his nickname while he
   - ☑ a. served in the navy. ✓
   - ☐ b. sat on a flagpole in Atlantic City.
   - ☐ c. was still in grammar school.

3. Kelly preferred flagpoles situated
   - ☐ a. at baseball fields.
   - ☐ b. near government buildings.
   - ☑ c. on hotel rooftops. ✓

4. Kelly set his all-time flagpole-sitting record at
   - ☑ a. Atlantic City. ✓
   - ☐ b. Newark.
   - ☐ c. Curtiss Field.

5. When Kelly died, he was holding under his arm
   - ☐ a. a miniature flagpole.
   - ☐ b. a portable radio.
   - ☑ c. old newspaper clippings. ✓

Score 5 points for each correct answer

__25__ TOTAL SCORE: Recalling Facts

C MAKING INFERENCES

An inference is a judgment that is made or an idea that is arrived at based on facts or on information that is given. You make an inference when you understand something that is *not* stated directly, but that is *implied*, or suggested by the facts that are given.

Below are five statements that are judgments or ideas that have been arrived at from the facts of the story. Write the letter C in the box in front of each statement that is a correct inference. Write the letter F in front of each faulty inference.

C—Correct Inference   F—Faulty Inference

✓ [F] 1. Shipwreck Kelly enjoyed privacy more than most people do.
[This is a *faulty* inference. He loved publicity and life in the limelight.]

✓ [C] 2. Shipwreck Kelly was not afraid of heights.
[This is a *correct* inference. No one afraid of heights would walk on the wing of a plane or sit for days on top of a flagpole.]

✓ [C] 3. Kelly had a good sense of balance.
[This is a *correct* inference. He needed a good sense of balance to sit for so long on the small disks he used on flagpoles and to take short naps without falling off.]

✓ [F] 4. Kelly's wife was also a flagpole sitter.
[This is a *faulty* inference. Kelly sat alone. His wife visited him once a week using a special chair.]

✓ [F] 5. Kelly always came down from flagpoles when it started to rain.
[This is a *faulty* inference. He had to expect some rain during his long stays on the tops of flagpoles, and never cut his stays short because of rain.]

Score 5 points for each correct answer

__25__ TOTAL SCORE: Making Inferences

D USING WORDS PRECISELY

Each of the numbered sentences below contains an underlined word or phrase from the story you have just read. Under the sentence are three definitions. One has the *same* meaning as the underlined word or phrase, one has *almost the same* meaning, and one has the *opposite* meaning. Match the definitions with the three answer choices by writing the letter that stands for each answer in the box in front of the definition it goes with.

S—Same   A—Almost the Same   O—Opposite

1. But Kelly's idea of getting a little fresh air was rather <u>offbeat</u>.

    ✓ [S] a. unusual

    ✓ [A] b. foreign

    ✓ [O] c. common

2. The 1920s were a fun-loving decade, filled with <u>loony</u> fads such as goldfish swallowing and marathon dancing.

    ✓ [A] a. odd

    ✓ [O] b. sensible

    ✓ [S] c. extremely silly

3. Thousands of people went by daily to witness the <u>implausible</u> stunt.

    ✓ [O] a. believable

    ✓ [S] b. incredible

    ✓ [A] c. unusual

4. Shipwreck Kelly slowly faded into <u>obscurity</u>.

    ✓ [S] a. forgotten state

    ✓ [A] b. privacy

    ✓ [O] c. fame

5. Tucked under his arm was a scrapbook filled with old newspaper clippings about the <u>exploits</u> of Alvin "Shipwreck" Kelly.

    ✓ [O] a. boring deeds

    ✓ [A] b. surprising moves

    ✓ [S] c. daring acts

<u>15</u> Score 3 points for each correct *S* answer
<u>10</u> Score 1 point for each correct *A* or *O* answer
<u>25</u> TOTAL SCORE: Using Words Precisely

● *Enter the four total scores in the spaces below, and add them together to find your Critical Reading Score. Then record your Critical Reading Score on the graph on page 157.*

_____ Finding the Main Idea
_____ Recalling Facts
_____ Making Inferences
_____ Using Words Precisely

_____ CRITICAL READING SCORE: Sample Unit

To the Student

It is often said that it takes all kinds to make a world. It is the differences among people that make life interesting. Well, if that's the case, some people are doing more than their share to keep the rest of us awake. People who act or think in offbeat ways are generally referred to as eccentrics. Eccentrics all have some highly individual way of viewing the world. Some concentrate their thoughts on strange ideas. Some do radical things to shake up the routine of everyday life. Some just act in ways that the rest of us find rather peculiar. All eccentrics do, however, have one thing in common: they break away from the ordinary paths of thought and action. *Eccentrics* brings you the stories of twenty-one people who demonstrate just how far-out human behavior can be.

While you are enjoying these compelling stories, you will be developing your reading skills. This book assumes that you already are a fairly good reader. *Eccentrics* is for students who want to read faster and to increase their understanding of what they read. If you complete all twenty-one units—reading the stories and completing the exercises—you will surely improve both your reading rate and your comprehension.

GROUP ONE

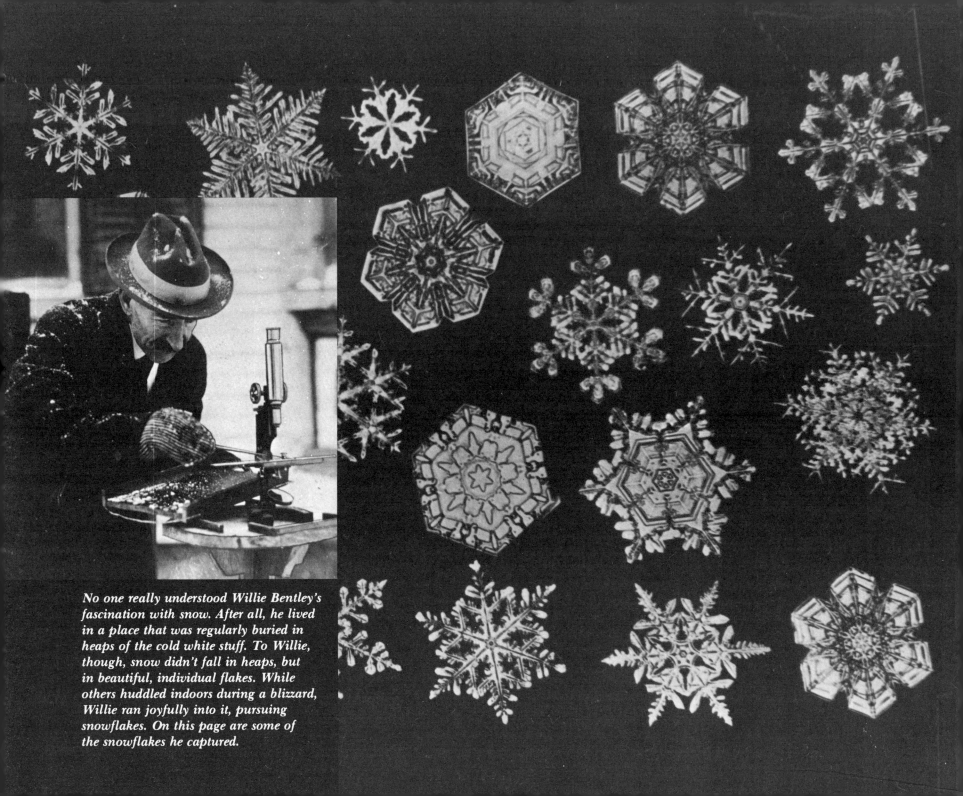

No one really understood Willie Bentley's fascination with snow. After all, he lived in a place that was regularly buried in heaps of the cold white stuff. To Willie, though, snow didn't fall in heaps, but in beautiful, individual flakes. While others huddled indoors during a blizzard, Willie ran joyfully into it, pursuing snowflakes. On this page are some of the snowflakes he captured.

Snowflake Bentley

The winter wind swept through the tiny village of Jericho, Vermont. Then the first snow of the 1880–1881 season began to fall. Most people took that as a good enough reason to stay inside. But Wilson "Willie" Bentley had other ideas. He pulled on his boots. Then he grabbed his coat, cap, and mittens and headed for the door.

Willie loved everything about the outdoors, but he especially loved the snow. Of course, other fifteen-year-olds loved snow too. But Willie's love went beyond sledding and snowball fights. He wanted to actually study the white stuff. So into the driving storm Willie trudged, carrying the new microscope his mother had given him. He caught a few snowflakes and placed them gently under his microscope. Looking down at them magnified thousands of times, Willie gasped. The snowflakes were all so beautiful, and they were all different. Their unique qualities, however, were lost forever when the snowflakes melted. Somehow, Willie thought, he had to capture their beauty.

At first Willie thought he could sketch each snowflake. So he set up a workshop in an unheated woodshed. He borrowed a piece of black velvet from his mother and used the swatch of fabric to catch snowflakes. After gathering a few prize samples, he would dash back to the woodshed and

place the snowflakes under his microscope. Then Willie would sketch as fast as he could. But he was never quite fast enough. The snowflake always melted before he could draw an accurate picture.

Willie's odd behavior caught everyone's attention. His father felt that Willie was wasting his time. Charlie, Willie's older brother, thought he was nuts. Most of the neighbors in Jericho shared that opinion. Still, Willie would not give up. He hoped that someday people would understand the beauty he saw in snowflakes. But for the moment his most urgent concern was finding a better way to preserve that beauty.

He spent hours striving to improve his sketches. Then one day he had a bright idea. He saw an advertisement for a special camera that could be attached to a microscope. With a camera like that, Willie thought, he could photograph snowflakes. He would then be able to keep a permanent record of each spectacular snowflake. Unfortunately, the camera cost a hundred dollars. In the 1880s, that was a lot of money to a poor farmer like Willie's father. Besides, what would the neighbors say? A man would have to be crazy to spend a hundred dollars so that his son could take pictures of snow.

Mr. Bentley wasn't crazy, and he still

couldn't make sense of his son's hobby, but he loved to see Willie happy. So he and his wife cut some corners to save money. Month after month they put aside a few dollars. On Willie's seventeenth birthday, Mr. and Mrs. Bentley presented their son with the special camera.

No one had ever photographed snowflakes before, so there were no books or manuals explaining how to go about it. Willie had to resort to trial and error. He tried one method after another. On January 15, 1885, he finally got it right. He took a perfect photograph of a snowflake.

Willie, who had come to be nicknamed Snowflake, wanted to do nothing but photograph snowflakes. And for the next forty-six years that is exactly what he did. He never married. He never moved from the farmhouse where he was born. Snowflake Bentley managed to survive by doing some farming and writing magazine articles. The money he made from the sale of his photos he spent on new equipment.

Willie lived for the next snowstorm. Townspeople got used to seeing him outdoors at the strangest hours and in the foulest weather. If it began snowing during mealtime, he would stop eating and dash outside. If a storm lasted all night, Willie would forget about sleeping. It seemed that he was always chasing one snowflake or another. He couldn't bear the thought that some great snowflake might escape his lens.

By 1931 Willie had photographed 5,381 snowflakes. People all over the world knew of his work. His book, *Snow Crystals,* was published in November 1931. Still, for Willie, now sixty-six years old, a new winter meant new snowflakes. In early December, he gave a lecture in a neighboring town. That night a terrible blizzard struck. Friends strongly urged Willie to stay in town. But Willie would have none of it. He loved wild snowstorms; they often yielded the best photos. So he wrapped a scarf around his neck and walked the six miles back to his house. When he finally staggered into his farmhouse, he was shaking all over.

The next day Willie fell ill. At first he insisted that he would get better. But he didn't. He only got worse. Finally Willie's nephew, who shared the farmhouse with him, called in the doctor. But it was too late. Snowflake Bentley died two days before Christmas. ■

If you have been timed while reading this selection, enter your reading time below. Then turn to the Words per Minute table on page 154 and look up your reading speed (words per minute). Enter your reading speed on the graph on page 156.

READING TIME: Unit 1

_____ : _____
Minutes   *Seconds*

How well did you read?

- *Answer the four types of questions that follow. The directions for each type of question tell you how to mark your answers.*

- *When you have finished all four exercises, check your work by using the answer key on page 150. For each right answer, put a check mark (✓) on the line beside the box. For each wrong answer, write the correct answer on the line.*

- *For scoring each exercise, follow the directions below the questions.*

A FINDING THE MAIN IDEA

Look at the three statements below. One expresses the main idea of the story you just read. A good main idea statement answers two questions: it tells *who* or *what* is the subject of the story, and it answers the understood question *does what?* or *is what?* Another statement is *too broad*, it is vague and doesn't tell much about the topic of the story. The third statement is *too narrow*, it tells about only one part of the story.

Match the statements with the three answer choices below by writing the letter of each answer in the box in front of the statement it goes with.

M—Main Idea   B—Too Broad   N—Too Narrow

_____ ☐ 1. Wilson "Snowflake" Bentley, who lived his whole life in Jericho, Vermont, loved snow.

_____ ☐ 2. Snowflake Bentley put together a book about snowflakes.

_____ ☐ 3. Wilson "Snowflake" Bentley devoted his life to capturing snowflakes on film.

_____ Score 15 points for a correct *M* answer

_____ Score 5 points for each correct *B* or *N* answer

_____ TOTAL SCORE: Finding the Main Idea

B RECALLING FACTS

How well do you remember the facts in the story you just read? Put an *x* in the box in front of the correct answer to each of the multiple choice questions below.

1. Willie set up his workshop in
   ___ ☐ a. the kitchen of his family's farmhouse.
   ___ ☐ b. an unheated woodshed.
   ___ ☐ c. a friend's house.

2. Wilson Bentley was the first person ever to
   ___ ☐ a. photograph snowflakes.
   ___ ☐ b. catch snowflakes.
   ___ ☐ c. walk six miles in a snowstorm.

3. Willie caught his snowflakes
   ___ ☐ a. in his hand.
   ___ ☐ b. on a cold piece of glass.
   ___ ☐ c. on a piece of black velvet.

4. Before getting his camera, Willie tried to preserve the beauty of snowflakes by
   ___ ☐ a. storing them on ice.
   ___ ☐ b. writing articles about them.
   ___ ☐ c. sketching them.

5. Willie never slept
   ___ ☐ a. when it was dark outside.
   ___ ☐ b. during a snowstorm.
   ___ ☐ c. more than four hours a night.

Score 5 points for each correct answer

___ TOTAL SCORE: Recalling Facts

C MAKING INFERENCES

An inference is a judgment that is made or an idea that is arrived at based on facts or on information that is given. You make an inference when you understand something that is *not* stated directly, but that is *implied,* or suggested by the facts that are given.

Below are five statements that are judgments or ideas that have been arrived at from the facts of the story. Write the letter *C* in the box in front of each statement that is a correct inference. Write the letter *F* in front of each faulty inference.

C—Correct Inference   F—Faulty Inference

___ ☐ 1. Almost everyone in Jericho, Vermont, knew Snowflake Bentley.

___ ☐ 2. Willie liked winters more than he liked summers.

___ ☐ 3. When photographing snowflakes, Willie often worked with partners.

___ ☐ 4. Snowflake Bentley was a lonely man.

___ ☐ 5. Snowflake Bentley died in poverty.

Score 5 points for each correct answer

___ TOTAL SCORE: Making Inferences

D USING WORDS PRECISELY

Each of the numbered sentences below contains an underlined word or phrase from the story you have just read. Under the sentence are three definitions. One has the *same* meaning as the underlined word or phrase, one has *almost the same* meaning, and one has the *opposite* meaning. Match the definitions with the three answer choices by writing the letter that stands for each answer in the box in front of the definition it goes with.

S—Same   A—Almost the Same   O—Opposite

1. The snowflakes always melted before he could draw an <u>accurate</u> picture.

   ____ ☐ a. correct

   ____ ☐ b. inexact

   ____ ☐ c. clear

2. He spent hours <u>striving</u> to improve his sketches.

   ____ ☐ a. trying

   ____ ☐ b. hoping

   ____ ☐ c. quitting

3. Willie had to <u>resort to</u> trial and error.

   ____ ☐ a. try

   ____ ☐ b. use

   ____ ☐ c. give up on

4. Townspeople got used to seeing him outdoors at the strangest hours and in the <u>foulest</u> weather.

   ____ ☐ a. nicest

   ____ ☐ b. coldest

   ____ ☐ c. nastiest

5. He loved wild snowstorms; they often <u>yielded</u> the best photos.

   ____ ☐ a. showed

   ____ ☐ b. provided

   ____ ☐ c. withheld

____ Score 3 points for each correct *S* answer

____ Score 1 point for each correct *A* or *O* answer

____ TOTAL SCORE: Using Words Precisely

• *Enter the four total scores in the spaces below, and add them together to find your Critical Reading Score. Then record your Critical Reading Score on the graph on page 157.*

> _____ Finding the Main Idea
> _____ Recalling Facts
> _____ Making Inferences
> _____ Using Words Precisely
> _____ CRITICAL READING SCORE: Unit 1

Jay Johnstone may never make it to the Hall of Fame, but he will long be remembered as one of the battiest players in baseball. Though he was a pretty good player, he just didn't take things seriously. To him, it seems, baseball was just a game.

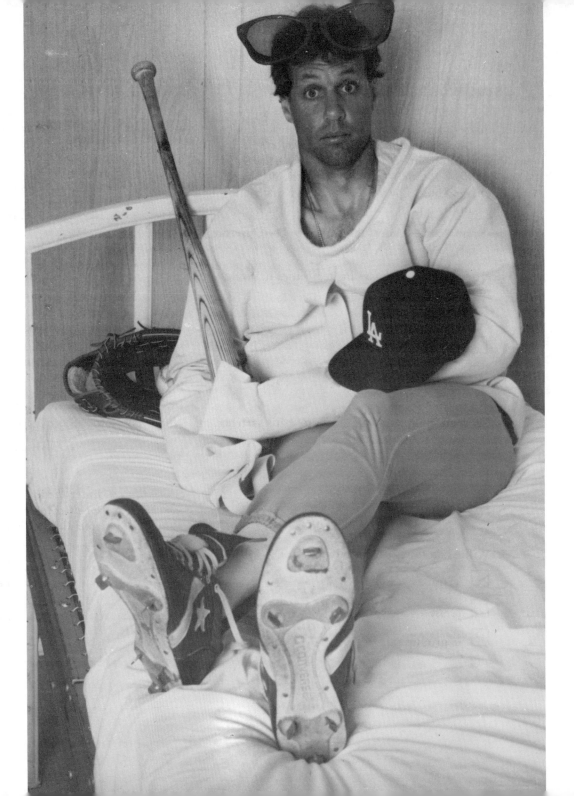

Jay Johnstone: Major League Clown

Other major league baseball players called him "Moon Man" or "Crazy Jay." They had good reason. Jay Johnstone once stuffed a soggy brownie into all-star Steve Garvey's glove. When a shortstop for the Los Angeles Dodgers made a couple of errors, Johnstone covered the man's glove with Band-Aids. He even ran pitcher Steve Howe's underwear up a flagpole in the ballpark. Johnstone loved to sit in the dugout wearing a beanie, giant sunglasses, or a space helmet. Sometimes he got hungry in the middle of a game. He thought nothing of leaving the dugout, in uniform, to go to the concession stand for a hot dog.

From 1966 to 1984, Jay Johnstone played major league baseball for eight different teams. Never a great player, he was good enough. He had to be to last as long as he did in the big leagues. In fact, for a couple of seasons he hit over .300. Still, Johnstone will not be remembered for his diving catches in the outfield or his clutch hitting. He will be remembered as one of the most hilarious jokesters ever to play baseball. And he will be remembered for the way he tormented other players and even his own manager.

Jay liked to do the unexpected. One day, while playing for the Los Angeles Dodgers, he decided to become a groundskeeper. Groundskeepers take care of the field. After the fifth inning of every game, they drag the infield with large metal rakes to remove cleat marks from the dirt. Jay and Dodger pitcher Jerry Reuss decided to join the crew.

Just before the fourth inning, Jay and Jerry slipped out of the dugout. No one saw them leave. They dashed down the corridor to the groundskeepers' room and quickly changed clothes. Then they gave two of the groundskeepers the night off. They persuaded the other two to go along with the gag. At the end of the fifth inning, Jay and Jerry proceeded to drag the infield along with the two regular groundskeepers. A TV cameraman spotted the players and covered their every move. The forty-seven thousand fans in the stands saw Jay and Jerry on the huge TV screen behind the left field wall. The crowd gave them a standing ovation.

Tommy Lasorda, the Dodgers manager, was not so pleased. When the men got back to the dugout, Lasorda slapped them each with a two hundred dollar fine for being out of uniform. But that was not all. Lasorda wanted to embarrass Johnstone. As Jay was scrambling back into his uniform, Lasorda ordered him to pinch-hit for the next batter. Fumbling with his shoes and belt, Jay grabbed a bat and headed for the plate. But it was Jay's night to shine. He whacked the ball over the rightfield fence for a home run. When he returned to the dugout, he shouted, "Hey Tommy, next time you need me, I'll be down in the groundskeepers' room."

Jay Johnstone loved to rile Tommy Lasorda. In 1981, the Dodgers beat the New York Yankees in the World Series. The next spring, the Dodgers were feeling pretty smug. Even Lasorda seemed to lack his usual grumpiness. One day Jay decided to liven things up a bit. He slipped into Lasorda's motel room and removed the speakers from the mouthpieces of both telephones. Then when Lasorda returned to his room around 2:00 A.M., Jay and catcher Steve Yeager rigged the door so he couldn't get out. They tied the doorknob to a palm tree in the hallway. Since the door opened inward, Lasorda was trapped. The next morning when he tried to go out for breakfast, he realized his predicament. He tried to call the operator for help. Of course, she couldn't hear him. Finally, Lasorda's screams brought help. By then, though, he had missed breakfast. That day Lasorda was his typical grumpy self.

Jay often rose to the defense of younger players. During the first half of the 1974 season, he played for the Toledo Mud Hens. They were the top minor league team from which the Philadelphia Phillies drew its players. (Jay had temporarily been sent down to the minors.) Jim Bunning managed the Mud Hens like an army drill sergeant. He wanted everyone to be perfect. When two young players went into a slump, Bunning called a team meeting. He berated the two players in front of the entire team. He told them they "were sinking faster than the *Titanic*." That incensed Jay. He felt that if the manager was going to blast a player, he should do it behind closed doors.

Naturally, Jay couldn't just leave it alone. The next day when he went to the outfield to shag fly balls, he was sporting a wet suit and a ski mask. Across his wet suit, Jay had taped in bold letters "USS Titanic." In case Bunning missed the point, Jay also carried an oar with him. He spent most of his warm-up time pretending to be paddling. When he headed for the infield, he dived into the turf as if he was trying to save himself from drowning.

Later that day, a TV crew showed up in the clubhouse. Pretending to be a commando, Jay crawled along the floor. He then lobbed a baseball into the manager's office as if it were a hand grenade. Bunning didn't think that was funny, either. He suspended Jay for thirty days. Crazy Jay never had to serve the suspension, however. A couple of days later, the Phillies called him back up to the major league club. Jay Johnstone was not only a little nutty, he was also rather lucky. ■

If you have been timed while reading this selection, enter your reading time below. Then turn to the Words per Minute table on page 154 and look up your reading speed (words per minute). Enter your reading speed on the graph on page 156.

READING TIME: Unit 2

_____ : _____
Minutes   *Seconds*

How well did you read?

- *Answer the four types of questions that follow. The directions for each type of question tell you how to mark your answers.*

- *When you have finished all four exercises, check your work by using the answer key on page 150. For each right answer, put a check mark (✔) on the line beside the box. For each wrong answer, write the correct answer on the line.*

- *For scoring each exercise, follow the directions below the questions.*

A FINDING THE MAIN IDEA

Look at the three statements below. One expresses the main idea of the story you just read. A good main idea statement answers two questions: it tells *who* or *what* is the subject of the story, and it answers the understood question *does what?* or *is what?* Another statement is *too broad*, it is vague and doesn't tell much about the topic of the story. The third statement is *too narrow*, it tells about only one part of the story.

Match the statements with the three answer choices below by writing the letter of each answer in the box in front of the statement it goes with.

M—Main Idea   B—Too Broad   N—Too Narrow

____ ☐ 1. Jay Johnstone was a baseball player who loved to play practical jokes.

____ ☐ 2. Jay Johnstone was an unusual baseball player.

____ ☐ 3. Jay Johnstone played major league baseball for eighteen years.

____ Score 15 points for a correct *M* answer
____ Score 5 points for each correct *B* or *N* answer

____ TOTAL SCORE: Finding the Main Idea

B RECALLING FACTS

How well do you remember the facts in the story you just read? Put an *x* in the box in front of the correct answer to each of the multiple choice questions below.

1. One of Jay's nicknames was
   ____ ☐ a. Moon Man.
   ____ ☐ b. The Hot Dog Man.
   ____ ☐ c. The USS *Titanic*.

2. After the fans saw Jay grooming the infield disguised as a groundskeeper, they
   ____ ☐ a. began to boo.
   ____ ☐ b. gave him a standing ovation.
   ____ ☐ c. put on giant sunglasses and beanies.

3. Tommy Lasorda was
   ____ ☐ a. Jay Johnstone's only friend.
   ____ ☐ b. manager of the Dodgers.
   ____ ☐ c. a catcher for the New York Yankees.

4. Jay locked Lasorda in a motel room by tying the doorknob to a
   ____ ☐ a. hand grenade.
   ____ ☐ b. huge TV screen.
   ____ ☐ c. palm tree in the hallway.

5. To show his displeasure with Jim Bunning, Johnstone once went to practice wearing
   ____ ☐ a. a wet suit and ski mask.
   ____ ☐ b. the uniform of an army drill sergeant.
   ____ ☐ c. an astronaut's space suit.

Score 5 points for each correct answer

____ TOTAL SCORE: Recalling Facts

C MAKING INFERENCES

An inference is a judgment that is made or an idea that is arrived at based on facts or on information that is given. You make an inference when you understand something that is *not* stated directly, but that is *implied*, or suggested by the facts that are given.

Below are five statements that are judgments or ideas that have been arrived at from the facts of the story. Write the letter *C* in the box in front of each statement that is a correct inference. Write the letter *F* in front of each faulty inference.

C—Correct Inference   F—Faulty Inference

____ ☐ 1. Jay Johnstone was an outfielder.

____ ☐ 2. Tommy Lasorda eventually threw Johnstone off the team for his antics.

____ ☐ 3. Ballplayers are not allowed to change out of their uniforms while the game is going on.

____ ☐ 4. Jay Johnstone was disliked by his fellow players for always trying to draw attention to himself.

____ ☐ 5. Jay always denied having played any practical jokes.

Score 5 points for each correct answer

____ TOTAL SCORE: Making Inferences

D USING WORDS PRECISELY

Each of the numbered sentences below contains an underlined word or phrase from the story you have just read. Under the sentence are three definitions. One has the *same* meaning as the underlined word or phrase, one has *almost the same* meaning, and one has the *opposite* meaning. Match the definitions with the three answer choices by writing the letter that stands for each answer in the box in front of the definition it goes with.

S—Same   A—Almost the Same   O—Opposite

1. Jay Johnstone loved to <u>rile</u> Tommy Lasorda.

 ____ ☐ a. please

 ____ ☐ b. irritate

 ____ ☐ c. outrage

2. The next morning when he tried to go out for breakfast, he realized his <u>predicament</u>.

 ____ ☐ a. difficult situation

 ____ ☐ b. crisis

 ____ ☐ c. good fortune

3. He <u>berated</u> the two players in front of the entire team.

 ____ ☐ a. complimented

 ____ ☐ b. scolded

 ____ ☐ c. criticized

4. That <u>incensed</u> Jay.

 ____ ☐ a. angered

 ____ ☐ b. pleased

 ____ ☐ c. annoyed

5. He then <u>lobbed</u> a baseball into the manager's office as if it were a hand grenade.

 ____ ☐ a. caught

 ____ ☐ b. dropped

 ____ ☐ c. tossed

____ Score 3 points for each correct S answer

____ Score 1 point for each correct A or O answer

____ **TOTAL SCORE: Using Words Precisely**

● *Enter the four total scores in the spaces below, and add them together to find your Critical Reading Score. Then record your Critical Reading Score on the graph on page 157.*

_____ Finding the Main Idea
_____ Recalling Facts
_____ Making Inferences
_____ Using Words Precisely

_____ **CRITICAL READING SCORE: Unit 2**

Black Bart had style—a peculiar style, but a style nonetheless. He was unlike any other bandit of the Old West. While desperados were shooting up the countryside, Bart went quietly and politely about his business of holding up stagecoaches. When he finally got caught, many people were sorry to see him punished.

Black Bart: Gentle Bandit

Charley Bolton was fed up. All his life he had struggled just to eke out a living. Though he loved his wife, Mary, and his three small daughters, he was tired of living in poverty. At the age of forty-five, he longed to start a new life. He wanted travel, excitement, and riches. So in 1875 Charley abandoned his family in Illinois and moved to California. He gave up his old values of honesty and hard work. He became Black Bart, the stagecoach robber. (Black Bart was a tough-sounding name he adopted for himself.)

Over the next eight years, Black Bart committed a total of twenty-eight robberies against the Wells Fargo Company. Not one of those robberies made him rich. By the 1870s, the California Gold Rush had ended. Wells Fargo stagecoaches no longer carried huge sums of cash. But although the holdups did not make Bart rich, they certainly did make him famous. By the time of his arrest in 1883, Black Bart was known throughout northern California.

Bart won his fame by capturing the imagination of the people. He approached crime in such an offbeat way that folks couldn't help but like him. For one thing, while most bandits worked with partners, Bart always worked alone. Although he carried a gun, he never fired a shot. He never even roughed anyone up. And while all other roadside bandits used horses to make their getaways, Bart worked on foot. After each holdup, he simply walked off into the woods. That led to many exaggerated stories about him. Some people claimed that he was a wild man who appeared out of nowhere and vanished into thin air. Some viewed him as an agent of the devil. Some even believed he was a ghost.

One other thing set Black Bart apart from all the other robbers of his era: his manners. During his holdups, Bart spoke politely. He waited patiently to collect the loot. Then he calmly told the stagecoach driver to go on with his route.

The robbery Bart committed on July 25, 1878, showed his special flair. For months he studied the stagecoach route, which ran through the mountains of north-central California. After much thought, he picked a spot for the holdup. It was a deserted place near a sharp bend in the road. Bart got to the spot bright and early. Dressed in a business suit and derby, he looked quite dapper.

Soon, though, he reached into his bag and pulled out a flour sack and a bathrobe. He slipped the bathrobe on over his suit. The flour sack, which had two eyeholes cut in it, he pulled over his hat and face. Clad in that ridiculous costume, Bart waited in the bushes until he heard the stage coming. Then he jumped into the middle of the road and pointed his rifle at the driver. Frightened, the driver brought the horses to a halt. "Throw down the box," Bart said softly.

The Wells Fargo box contained all the money and mail to be delivered that day. The driver did as Bart asked. When Bart had the box in his hand, he spoke to the driver again. "All right," he said, "you may drive on."

As the stagecoach thundered out of sight, Bart gave a friendly wave to the startled driver. Then he pulled an ax from his bag and chopped open the Wells Fargo box. Inside he found six hundred dollars. Bart scooped up the money and put it in his bag. Next he took off the bathrobe and flour sack and stuffed those in the bag too. Finally, Bart grabbed a piece of mail from the Wells Fargo box and took out a pencil. Impulsively, he wrote a short poem on the back of the envelope. It read:

Yet come what will, I'll try it once
My condition can't be worse;
And if there's money in that box
Tis money in my purse.

He signed it "Black Bart, the Po 8."
With a smile on his face, Bart put the

poem back in the box. It would be his gift to the detectives who tried to track him down. Then Bart picked up his bags and headed off through the mountains. He walked for several hours before reaching a small town. In the town he introduced himself as a traveling businessman. He then caught a ride to a distant city, far from the scene of the crime.

As word of the robberies spread, Bart became more and more popular. The soft voice, the silly disguise, and the poems made him a hot topic of conversation. Black Bart continued his life of well-mannered crime until November 3, 1883, when he finally met up with a piece of bad luck. He held up a stagecoach bound for Milton, California. By that time the Wells Fargo company had started bolting its boxes to the floors of stage-coaches in hopes of discouraging bandits like Black Bart. It didn't work. Bart simply climbed into the stagecoach and chopped the box open. Before he got started, he ordered the driver to unhitch the horses and take them down the road. He told the driver to wait there until he'd finished the robbery.

As luck would have it, on this particular day a young boy was hunting in the nearby woods. Seeing the driver and horses waiting around in the road, the boy realized what was happening. Quietly he joined the driver, and the two of them crept back to the stagecoach. By the time they reached it, Bart had collected the money and was heading into the woods. The boy quickly took aim with his hunting rifle and fired. The bullet nicked Bart, causing him to drop the money bag.

Bart managed to escape into the woods, but the damage had been done. When the Wells Fargo detective examined the contents of the bag, he found a handkerchief. The handkerchief had a laundry mark. Using that clue, the detective tracked down the owner. A week later, in San Francisco, the police arrested the infamous Black Bart.

At first Bart denied everything. Under persistent questioning, though, he finally confessed. When he'd told his story to the police, newspaper reporters across the state wrote articles glorifying him. Still, the court found Bart guilty and sentenced him to six years at San Quentin Prison. Before being led away, however, Black Bart told the judge one last thing. He had never wanted to hurt anyone. It was true he had used a rifle, but it had never been loaded. ■

If you have been timed while reading this selection, enter your reading time below. Then turn to the Words per Minute table on page 154 and look up your reading speed (words per minute). Enter your reading speed on the graph on page 156.

READING TIME: Unit 3
_____ : _____
Minutes   *Seconds*

How well did you read?

- *Answer the four types of questions that follow. The directions for each type of question tell you how to mark your answers.*

- *When you have finished all four exercises, check your work by using the answer key on page 150. For each right answer, put a check mark (✓) on the line beside the box. For each wrong answer, write the correct answer on the line.*

- *For scoring each exercise, follow the directions below the questions.*

A FINDING THE MAIN IDEA

Look at the three statements below. One expresses the main idea of the story you just read. A good main idea statement answers two questions: it tells *who* or *what* is the subject of the story, and it answers the understood question *does what?* or *is what?* Another statement is *too broad*, it is vague and doesn't tell much about the topic of the story. The third statement is *too narrow*, it tells about only one part of the story.

Match the statements with the three answer choices below by writing the letter of each answer in the box in front of the statement it goes with.

M—Main Idea   **B—Too Broad**   **N—Too Narrow**

_____ ☐ 1. Black Bart left his home and family to become a stagecoach robber.

_____ ☐ 2. Black Bart became famous as a polite, colorful, and nonviolent stagecoach robber.

_____ ☐ 3. Black Bart was a famous robber in the late 1800s.

_____ Score 15 points for a correct *M* answer

_____ Score 5 points for each correct *B* or *N* answer

_____ TOTAL SCORE: Finding the Main Idea

B RECALLING FACTS

How well do you remember the facts in the story you just read? Put an *x* in the box in front of the correct answer to each of the multiple choice questions below.

1. When Black Bart committed a robbery, he always worked
   - ____ ☐ a. with two partners.
   - ____ ☐ b. alone.
   - ____ ☐ c. on horseback.

2. Black Bart left a poem
   - ____ ☐ a. on the driver's seat of a stagecoach.
   - ____ ☐ b. in the saddlebag of a horse.
   - ____ ☐ c. in a Wells Fargo box.

3. Bart committed his robberies wearing
   - ____ ☐ a. women's clothing.
   - ____ ☐ b. a bathrobe.
   - ____ ☐ c. a clown suit.

4. The clue that finally led to the capture of Black Bart was a
   - ____ ☐ a. laundry mark on a handkerchief.
   - ____ ☐ b. poem that Black Bart left on an envelope.
   - ____ ☐ c. bullet that matched the gun Black Bart used.

5. After his trial, Black Bart was
   - ____ ☐ a. released.
   - ____ ☐ b. sentenced to six years in prison.
   - ____ ☐ c. sent back to Illinois.

Score 5 points for each correct answer

____ TOTAL SCORE: Recalling Facts

C MAKING INFERENCES

An inference is a judgment that is made or an idea that is arrived at based on facts or on information that is given. You make an inference when you understand something that is *not* stated directly, but that is *implied,* or suggested by the facts that are given.

Below are five statements that are judgments or ideas that have been arrived at from the facts of the story. Write the letter *C* in the box in front of each statement that is a correct inference. Write the letter *F* in front of each faulty inference.

C—Correct Inference   F—Faulty Inference

- ____ ☐ 1. During the California Gold Rush, Wells Fargo stagecoaches carried huge sums of cash.

- ____ ☐ 2. To Black Bart, adventure was more important than family.

- ____ ☐ 3. Black Bart was one of the most feared robbers of his day.

- ____ ☐ 4. Black Bart lived by himself in the woods.

- ____ ☐ 5. Black Bart enjoyed his life as a stagecoach robber.

Score 5 points for each correct answer

____ TOTAL SCORE: Making Inferences

D USING WORDS PRECISELY

Each of the numbered sentences below contains an underlined word or phrase from the story you have just read. Under the sentence are three definitions. One has the *same* meaning as the underlined word or phrase, one has *almost the same* meaning, and one has the *opposite* meaning. Match the definitions with the three answer choices by writing the letter that stands for each answer in the box in front of the definition it goes with.

S—Same   A—Almost the Same   O—Opposite

1. Dressed in a business suit and derby, he looked quite dapper.

___ ☐ a. dowdy

___ ☐ b. stylish

___ ☐ c. presentable

2. Impulsively, he wrote a short poem on the back of the envelope.

___ ☐ a. on the spur of the moment

___ ☐ b. after much planning

___ ☐ c. in a careless way

3. A week later, in San Francisco, the police arrested the infamous Black Bart.

___ ☐ a. noted

___ ☐ b. having a bad reputation

___ ☐ c. evil

4. Under persistent questioning, though, he finally confessed.

___ ☐ a. quick and short

___ ☐ b. unending

___ ☐ c. continued

5. When he'd told his story to the police, newspaper reporters across the state wrote articles glorifying him.

___ ☐ a. celebrating

___ ☐ b. worshiping

___ ☐ c. condemning

___ Score 3 points for each correct S answer

___ Score 1 point for each correct A or O answer

___ TOTAL SCORE: Using Words Precisely

• *Enter the four total scores in the spaces below, and add them together to find your Critical Reading Score. Then record your Critical Reading Score on the graph on page 157.*

_____ Finding the Main Idea
_____ Recalling Facts
_____ Making Inferences
_____ Using Words Precisely

_____ CRITICAL READING SCORE: Unit 3

George Kaufman was a big believer in germs—and in avoiding them. He relied heavily on his doctors and on medicine to keep him healthy, and he relied on them constantly. He believed that good health was a shaky thing, and that one could never be too protective of it—something could get you when you least expect it.

George Kaufman: Keeping Fit

George Kaufman hated doorknobs. To be more accurate, he feared doorknobs. He feared the dirt that built up on them. He feared the fingerprints that people left on them. Above all, he feared the diseases he believed he could catch from them. As a young man, Kaufman became convinced that all doorknobs were dirty. As he saw it, an average doorknob collected germs from dozens of unclean hands every day. So he went through life avoiding contact with the filthy things. He never put his bare hand on a doorknob. When he needed to open a door, he would stick his hand into his jacket pocket and, with the fabric protecting him, grab the doorknob.

Luckily, his fear did not interfere with his work. From 1920 until his death in 1961, Kaufman wrote more than forty Broadway plays. They included such smash hits as *Dinner at Eight, You Can't Take It with You,* and *The Man Who Came to Dinner.* Despite his success, though, Kaufman remained a man plagued by fears. His fear of doorknobs was not an isolated quirk. He also dreaded dust, horses, cheese, roast goose, foreign countries, and many other things. He despised everything that struck him as unclean. He hated shaking hands. He could picture thousands of tiny germs jumping from the other person's hand onto his. He loathed eating in restaurants because he could never be sure the silverware had been sterilized. He disliked eating at friends' houses for the same reason.

Kaufman's fears all stemmed from the same source. He was uncommonly worried about his health. Kaufman had no real health problems until he was in his late fifties. But that didn't matter. The point was that he believed he had problems. His fears caused him real anguish. Sometimes he focused on his teeth. It seemed to him that they were about to fall out. To reassure himself, he saw his dentist at least six times a year. He also became preoccupied with his eyes. He was sure he was going blind. To avoid eyestrain, he bought several different pairs of glasses. Whenever he needed to refocus his vision, he would change glasses.

Because Kaufman was rich, famous, and successful, many people did not realize the depth of his fears. But every day, day after day, he tortured himself with his thoughts. He would not go near open windows, fearing that a sudden chill would injure his lungs. He always took his own breakfast cereal with him when traveling. He feared that the chefs of even the best hotels might contaminate the food.

To Kaufman, the world seemed fraught with danger. He had nightmares in which he developed ulcers, heart trouble, cancer. If a friend had a bad cough, he assumed that he would catch it. In fact, he would begin preparing for a serious lung disease. If someone had a headache, Kaufman's head would begin to throb. Within hours he would have himself convinced that he had a brain tumor.

Kaufman sometimes tried to hide his worries by making jokes. He once made a humorous remark about a man who was a year older than he. "I watch him very carefully," Kaufman said, "to see what I'm going to catch next year." Most people laughed at that line, not guessing that it contained a great deal of truth.

In an effort to protect his health, Kaufman put himself in the care of all kinds of medical specialists. He had doctors looking out for his feet, his back, and his internal organs. He hired one doctor to tend to his nervous system. He hired another to keep tabs on his circulation. He hired a third to provide psychiatric counseling. He even hired a specialist to give him treatments to prevent baldness.

Kaufman felt he could not survive without his doctors. But that did not mean he treated them well. He was often demanding and unreasonable with them. He resented any personal questions they asked. He refused to accept their diagnoses that he was healthy. He insisted that they give him injections even though he wasn't sick. As long as he was getting a shot, he felt he was being helped.

Once, late on a Sunday night, Kaufman called Dr. Menard Gertler. Gertler had just become Kaufman's personal physician. "I need you immediately," Kaufman said when Gertler answered the phone. Then Kaufman hung up. Gertler grabbed his medical bag and rushed out the door. Arriving at Kaufman's apartment building, he announced that there was a medical emergency in Kaufman's apartment. He asked the elevator operator to take him up directly. When Gertler burst into Kaufman's room, however, he found his patient standing in the middle of the floor, holding a stopwatch in his hand. Shocked, Gertler asked for an explanation. Said Kaufman calmly, "I wanted to see how long it would take you to get here if I were *really* ill." ■

If you have been timed while reading this selection, enter your reading time below. Then turn to the Words per Minute table on page 154 and look up your reading speed (words per minute). Enter your reading speed on the graph on page 156.

READING TIME: Unit 4

_____ : _____
Minutes   *Seconds*

How well did you read?

- *Answer the four types of questions that follow. The directions for each type of question tell you how to mark your answers.*

- *When you have finished all four exercises, check your work by using the answer key on page 150. For each right answer, put a check mark (✔) on the line beside the box. For each wrong answer, write the correct answer on the line.*

- *For scoring each exercise, follow the directions below the questions.*

A FINDING THE MAIN IDEA

Look at the three statements below. One expresses the main idea of the story you just read. A good main idea statement answers two questions: it tells *who* or *what* is the subject of the story, and it answers the understood question *does what?* or *is what?* Another statement is *too broad*, it is vague and doesn't tell much about the topic of the story. The third statement is *too narrow*, it tells about only one part of the story.

Match the statements with the three answer choices below by writing the letter of each answer in the box in front of the statement it goes with.

M—Main Idea   **B—Too Broad**   **N—Too Narrow**

_____ ☐ 1. George Kaufman was an American playwright who wrote more than forty Broadway plays.

_____ ☐ 2. George Kaufman's life was dominated by a fear of germs and diseases.

_____ ☐ 3. George Kaufman lived a life filled with fear.

_____ Score 15 points for a correct *M* answer

_____ Score 5 points for each correct *B* or *N* answer

_____ TOTAL SCORE: Finding the Main Idea

B RECALLING FACTS

How well do you remember the facts in the story you just read? Put an *x* in the box in front of the correct answer to each of the multiple choice questions below.

1. Kaufman always kept his hand in his jacket pocket when
   - ____ ☐ a. shaking hands.
   - ____ ☐ b. opening doors.
   - ____ ☐ c. eating.

2. Kaufman feared he
   - ____ ☐ a. had no true friends.
   - ____ ☐ b. was going blind.
   - ____ ☐ c. would lose the ability to write good plays.

3. When traveling, Kaufman always brought along his own
   - ____ ☐ a. breakfast cereal.
   - ____ ☐ b. silverware.
   - ____ ☐ c. medical books.

4. Kaufman had nightmares in which
   - ____ ☐ a. he was chased by giant doorknobs.
   - ____ ☐ b. his teeth fell out.
   - ____ ☐ c. he developed cancer.

5. Kaufman did not like his doctors to
   - ____ ☐ a. give him shots.
   - ____ ☐ b. tell him bad news.
   - ____ ☐ c. ask him personal questions.

Score 5 points for each correct answer

____ TOTAL SCORE: Recalling Facts

C MAKING INFERENCES

An inference is a judgment that is made or an idea that is arrived at based on facts or on information that is given. You make an inference when you understand something that is *not* stated directly, but that is *implied*, or suggested by the facts that are given.

Below are five statements that are judgments or ideas that have been arrived at from the facts of the story. Write the letter *C* in the box in front of each statement that is a correct inference. Write the letter *F* in front of each faulty inference.

C—Correct Inference   F—Faulty Inference

- ____ ☐ 1. Kaufman thought that most doctors were quacks.
- ____ ☐ 2. Kaufman had many friends who were seriously ill.
- ____ ☐ 3. Kaufman felt that horses were unclean.
- ____ ☐ 4. After Kaufman called him for nothing, Dr. Gertler resigned as his personal physician.
- ____ ☐ 5. Kaufman lived in the city.

Score 5 points for each correct answer

____ TOTAL SCORE: Making Inferences

D USING WORDS PRECISELY

Each of the numbered sentences below contains an underlined word or phrase from the story you have just read. Under the sentence are three definitions. One has the *same* meaning as the underlined word or phrase, one has *almost the same* meaning, and one has the *opposite* meaning. Match the definitions with the three answer choices by writing the letter that stands for each answer in the box in front of the definition it goes with.

S—Same   A—Almost the Same   O—Opposite

1. His fear of doorknobs was not an isolated <u>quirk</u>.

____ ☐ a. peculiarity

____ ☐ b. common trait

____ ☐ c. abnormality

2. He <u>loathed</u> eating in restaurants because he could never be sure the silverware had been sterilized.

____ ☐ a. loved

____ ☐ b. disliked

____ ☐ c. hated

3. His fears caused him real <u>anguish</u>.

____ ☐ a. sorrow

____ ☐ b. distress

____ ☐ c. comfort

4. He feared that the chefs of even the best hotels might <u>contaminate</u> the food.

____ ☐ a. purify

____ ☐ b. pollute

____ ☐ c. spoil

5. To Kaufman, the world seemed <u>fraught</u> with danger.

____ ☐ a. loaded

____ ☐ b. lacking

____ ☐ c. overrun

____ Score 3 points for each correct *S* answer
____ Score 1 point for each correct *A* or *O* answer

____ TOTAL SCORE: Using Words Precisely

- *Enter the four total scores in the spaces below, and add them together to find your Critical Reading Score. Then record your Critical Reading Score on the graph on page 157.*

_____ Finding the Main Idea
_____ Recalling Facts
_____ Making Inferences
_____ Using Words Precisely

_____ CRITICAL READING SCORE: Unit 4

John Chapman had no permanent home and no family of his own. He chose to live close to the land, for he loved the growing things and the creatures of the earth. He traveled the countryside, leaving his own special gift behind for the pioneers who were settling the land.

Johnny Appleseed

John Chapman wasn't what you'd call a snappy dresser. In fact, he often dressed in old coffee sacks and walked around with a pan tied to his head. Even during the frontier days of the United States, when settlers lived a rough and simple life, he was quite a sight.

In the early 1800s, pioneer families often spotted Johnny trudging across snowy fields or following the banks of a river. He slept on the ground and ate whatever nuts or berries he could find. A light traveler, he carried only two sacks with him. The smaller one held all his possessions. The larger one contained hundreds of thousands of apple seeds. It was those apple seeds that earned him the nickname Johnny Appleseed.

Johnny began planting apple seeds in 1801. He was twenty-six years old at the time, and eager to help extend the western boundary of the United States. To most people, extending the frontier meant moving out to the Midwest and settling down to live in Indiana, Michigan, or Ohio. It meant building homes, schools, and roads. It meant battling hostile Indians and stalking wild game. But Johnny Appleseed did not think or act like other people. He wanted to pave the way for settlers by planting apple trees. Johnny believed the presence of the fruit-bearing

trees would make life easier for settlers. The fragrance of the blossoms would lift the spirits of weary pioneers. The beauty of the trees would be a living symbol of God's love, he thought. In addition, the apples would have practical uses. Settlers could make applesauce, apple pies, apple dumplings, and apple butter. They could make apple vinegar as a preservative for vegetables. And they could make apple brandy.

Armed with only his good intentions and his sack full of seeds, he set out for the western wilderness. For fifty years he wandered the frontier, digging little holes and dropping in apple seeds. He did try settling down from time to time, and often spent winters with his sister's family in Ohio. But sooner or later he would get restless. So he would take off again, his bag of seeds slung over his shoulder. On each trip, he tried to plant as many seeds as possible. Sometimes he fenced off two or three acres of land and planted a small orchard. He liked to return to those orchards every few years to check on the progress of the saplings.

His journeys afforded him plenty of time to study nature. And the more he studied it, the more he loved it. In fact, Johnny got a little carried away. He got so he couldn't bear the thought of harming

any living creature. If he saw a bug heading toward his campfire, he quickly doused the flames to save the insect. He even worried that the smoke from his fire might choke an innocent mosquito. One time he accidentally stepped on a worm. When he realized what he had done, a look of horror spread across his face. After mourning the death of the worm, he decided to punish that killer foot of his. He headed for a path strewn with sharp stones. Then he took off his shoe and made the offending foot walk barefoot for several miles.

Clearly, a man like Johnny wouldn't consider eating meat or wearing clothes made of animal skin or fur. He also refused to ride a horse because he felt that that would be cruel to the animal. In fact, he regularly came to the aid of old broken-down horses. He couldn't stand to see them abused or turned loose to die in the forests, so he bought them, raising the necessary money by doing odd jobs. Then he persuaded friends to care for them while he continued his travels. Johnny showed equal concern for the health and comfort of his apple trees. Although he picked apples, he could never bring himself to prune a branch.

Naturally, most people thought Johnny was a little weird. They wondered aloud if perhaps he had been kicked in the head by a horse. He had, as one man described it, a "thick bark of queerness on him." Still, people had to admire his toughness. If his shoes wore out in the middle of winter, he didn't care. He just kept walking over the icy ground until he found a pair that some settler had discarded. If he hurt himself, he would treat the wound by burning it with a hot piece of iron. As painful as that method was, it did seal the wound. Then Johnny merely had to deal with a third-degree burn.

Johnny always felt completely at ease in the wilderness. He thought of bears and wolves and poisonous snakes as his friends. He didn't worry about Indians, either. He treated all Indians with such gentleness that they never dreamed of harming him. According to legend, Johnny was so relaxed that he could fall asleep anywhere. It is said that he once dozed off in his canoe and didn't wake up until he had drifted a hundred miles downstream. On another occasion, a group of Seneca Indians mistook him for an enemy and began chasing him. As the story goes, Johnny slipped into a swamp and lay down so that only his mouth was above water. Then he drifted peacefully off to sleep, waking up long after the warriors had passed.

In 1844, at the age of seventy, Johnny Appleseed was still going strong. Then, in March of 1845, he made his last journey. Hearing that cattle had broken down one of his orchard fences, he set out on a fifteen-mile hike through the snow to repair it. Along the way he caught pneumonia. Johnny Appleseed died a few days later. The trees he had planted remained a monument to him, forming the core of many of the country's best and most beautiful orchards. ■

If you have been timed while reading this selection, enter your reading time below. Then turn to the Words per Minute table on page 154 and look up your reading speed (words per minute). Enter your reading speed on the graph on page 156.

READING TIME: Unit 5

_____ : _____
Minutes   Seconds

How well did you read?

- *Answer the four types of questions that follow. The directions for each type of question tell you how to mark your answers.*

- *When you have finished all four exercises, check your work by using the answer key on page 150. For each right answer, put a check mark (✓) on the line beside the box. For each wrong answer, write the correct answer on the line.*

- *For scoring each exercise, follow the directions below the questions.*

A FINDING THE MAIN IDEA

Look at the three statements below. One expresses the main idea of the story you just read. A good main idea statement answers two questions: it tells *who* or *what* is the subject of the story, and it answers the understood question *does what?* or *is what?* Another statement is *too broad,* it is vague and doesn't tell much about the topic of the story. The third statement is *too narrow,* it tells about only one part of the story.

Match the statements with the three answer choices below by writing the letter of each answer in the box in front of the statement it goes with.

M—Main Idea   **B—Too Broad**   **N—Too Narrow**

____ ☐ 1. Johnny Appleseed planted thousands of apple trees in the Midwest.

____ ☐ 2. Johnny Appleseed lived a wandering life.

____ ☐ 3. Johnny Appleseed loved and respected all of nature, and traveled the frontier planting apple seeds.

____ Score 15 points for a correct *M* answer

____ Score 5 points for each correct *B* or *N* answer

____ TOTAL SCORE: Finding the Main Idea

B RECALLING FACTS

How well do you remember the facts in the story you just read?
Put an *x* in the box in front of the correct answer to each of the
multiple choice questions below.

1. Johnny Appleseed did not eat
   - ____ ☐ a. meat.
   - ____ ☐ b. apples.
   - ____ ☐ c. vegetables.

2. Johnny often spent winters with
   - ____ ☐ a. the Seneca Indians.
   - ____ ☐ b. friends in Boston, Massachusetts.
   - ____ ☐ c. his sister's family in Ohio.

3. Johnny collected old broken-down
   - ____ ☐ a. shoes.
   - ____ ☐ b. horses.
   - ____ ☐ c. fences.

4. Johnny treated his wounds by
   - ____ ☐ a. burning them with a hot piece of iron.
   - ____ ☐ b. soaking them in swamp water.
   - ____ ☐ c. rubbing apple juice into them.

5. The last trip Johnny took was a
   - ____ ☐ a. fifteen-mile hike through the snow.
   - ____ ☐ b. horseback ride over the mountains.
   - ____ ☐ c. journey to visit his sister.

Score 5 points for each correct answer

____ TOTAL SCORE: Recalling Facts

C MAKING INFERENCES

An inference is a judgment that is made or an idea that is
arrived at based on facts or on information that is given. You
make an inference when you understand something that is *not*
stated directly, but that is *implied*, or suggested by the facts that
are given.

Below are five statements that are judgments or ideas that
have been arrived at from the facts of the story. Write the letter
C in the box in front of each statement that is a correct inference. Write the letter *F* in front of each faulty inference.

C—Correct Inference   F—Faulty Inference

- ____ ☐ 1. No one in Johnny's family ate meat or wore clothes made from animal fur.

- ____ ☐ 2. Johnny Appleseed was basically lazy.

- ____ ☐ 3. Johnny Appleseed planted more apple trees than anyone else in his day.

- ____ ☐ 4. Pruning branches will kill an apple tree.

- ____ ☐ 5. Johnny Appleseed didn't feel that personal appearance was of great importance.

Score 5 points for each correct answer

____ TOTAL SCORE: Making Inferences

D USING WORDS PRECISELY

Each of the numbered sentences below contains an underlined word or phrase from the story you have just read. Under the sentence are three definitions. One has the *same* meaning as the underlined word or phrase, one has *almost the same* meaning, and one has the *opposite* meaning. Match the definitions with the three answer choices by writing the letter that stands for each answer in the box in front of the definition it goes with.

S—Same   **A—Almost the Same**   **O—Opposite**

1. If he saw a bug heading toward his campfire, he quickly <u>doused</u> the flames to save the insect from a painful burn.

___ ☐ a. lit

___ ☐ b. stopped

___ ☐ c. extinguished

2. He headed for a path <u>strewn</u> with sharp stones.

___ ☐ a. scattered

___ ☐ b. filled

___ ☐ c. paved

3. He just kept walking over the icy ground until he found another pair that some settler had <u>discarded</u>.

___ ☐ a. put aside

___ ☐ b. thrown away

___ ☐ c. picked up

4. His journeys <u>afforded</u> him plenty of time to study nature.

___ ☐ a. provided

___ ☐ b. set aside

___ ☐ c. took away

5. Then he took off his shoe and made the <u>offending</u> foot walk barefoot for several miles.

___ ☐ a. guilty

___ ☐ b. causing injury

___ ☐ c. helpful

___ Score 3 points for each correct *S* answer

___ Score 1 point for each correct *A* or *O* answer

___ **TOTAL SCORE:** Using Words Precisely

● *Enter the four total scores in the spaces below, and add them together to find your Critical Reading Score. Then record your Critical Reading Score on the graph on page 157.*

_____ Finding the Main Idea
_____ Recalling Facts
_____ Making Inferences
_____ Using Words Precisely
_____ **CRITICAL READING SCORE: Unit 5**

Jim Brady's wardrobe glittered. On his shirtfront, cuffs, and fingers, impressive rocks caught the light, broke it into thousands of tiny, shimmering pieces, and threw it back to deliver the message that Jim Brady was rich. He liked being rich. He liked people to know he was rich. But though his love of diamonds was noteworthy, it didn't reflect his greatest eccentricity: more than anything, Diamond Jim Brady loved food.

Diamond Jim Brady

"If you're going to make money, you have to look like money." James Buchanan Brady said it, and he believed every word. Brady, a nineteenth-century millionaire, liked to show off his fancy clothes. He acquired a vast wardrobe that included two hundred custom-made suits and fifty silk hats. Mostly, though, Brady loved diamonds. He felt that a man without diamonds was a man without power.

Brady believed that diamonds impressed people, and he wanted to impress. He carried a handful of diamonds around in his pocket. No one in New York City ever saw larger diamond rings than the ones Brady wore. He even had an enormous diamond set in the top of his cane. He wore diamond cuff links and diamond shirt studs and diamond watches. He once bought his girlfriend a gold-plated bicycle and had a string of diamonds embedded in the handlebars. Brady never apologized for his extravagant spending habits. And he gloried in his well-earned nickname, Diamond Jim.

Brady didn't start out in life surrounded by diamonds. He grew up in a poor working-class section of New York City. As a boy, he worked in his father's saloon. But young Brady loathed the saloon. In 1867, at the age of eleven, he ran away from home. Within a few years, he got a job selling equipment for the New York Central Railroad. It seemed that Brady could sell anything to anyone. Before reaching the age of thirty, he had amassed a sizable fortune. He could afford anything he wanted. He could buy diamonds and fine clothes, and he could eat in all the best restaurants.

If Brady had a weakness for diamonds, he had an even greater weakness for food. He may just have been the all-time American eating champion. His appetite knew no bounds. After fleeing his father's saloon, young Brady first went to work at New York's St. James Hotel as a bellhop. Free food came with the job. But Brady ate so much that the hotel made a new rule. Jim Brady could not eat at the employees' free lunch bar.

As a wealthy man, Diamond Jim could eat all he wanted. And he ate enough to kill most people. In fact, some of his friends wondered why he didn't drop dead in the middle of one of his colossal meals. Take a look at his typical breakfast: He began with a large steak, pork chops, and a plateful of eggs. Then he downed a stack of pancakes, fried potatoes, corn bread, and a half dozen muffins. He washed everything down with a pitcher of milk and a gallon of orange juice. This breakfast he viewed as a light snack just to get him going. He saved his serious eating for later in the day.

Around eleven thirty in the morning, Diamond Jim liked to snack on two or three dozen oysters. He insisted on having oysters every day. During the summer, he often stayed at the Manhattan Beach Hotel in New York. After breakfast, Diamond Jim would go for a swim in the pool. The hotel's waiters would watch to see when he came out of the water. Then they would scurry around madly to get a huge platter of chilled, freshly-opened oysters ready by the time Brady set foot on the hotel porch.

At twelve thirty every day, Brady had lunch. His usual fare included two broiled lobsters, more oysters, and deviled crabs. That would be followed up by a large steak and a few pieces of fruit pie. For dessert, Diamond Jim would consume a two-pound box of chocolates. He said that the chocolates helped to settle his stomach.

In just two meals, Diamond Jim had eaten enough food to keep the average person going for a week. But everything he had consumed to that point was just a warm-up for dinner. Diamond Jim often dined at Charles Rector's in New York City. The owner once boasted that Brady was "the best twenty-five customers" he had. People who saw Diamond Jim eat dinner would swear that he ate like a man who hadn't seen food in weeks.

Diamond Jim especially loved seafood. He usually began dinner with around thirty oysters. Then he would feast on a half dozen crabs before wolfing down two bowls of green turtle soup. Only then would he move on to the main courses. An average Brady dinner included six lobsters, a couple of ducks, steak, and vegetables. Diamond Jim followed that with a tray full of pastries and his customary two-pound box of chocolates. As usual, he washed down his banquet with several quarts of orange juice. He never drank coffee, tea, or alcohol.

Brady clearly liked large quantities of food. But he didn't go for bulk alone; he prized high-quality treats. Once he sampled a box of chocolates from Page and Shaw, a small Boston candymaker. Claiming it was the best candy he'd ever tasted, Diamond Jim ordered several hundred boxes for himself and his friends. The candymakers, however, couldn't fill the order. Their plant was too small. Without a pause, Diamond Jim wrote out an interest-free loan for $150,000. He told the candymakers to double the size of their plant. They could repay him with chocolates.

On another occasion, Diamond Jim became obsessed with a fish sauce he'd tried in Paris. Only one restaurant in the world made it, and the recipe was a closely guarded secret. But Charles Rector wanted nothing more than to please his favorite customer. So he took his son out of law school and sent him to Paris to steal the recipe.

Under an assumed name, the young man got a job washing pots at the Paris restaurant. Slowly he worked his way up to assistant chef. It took him several months, but he finally got the recipe. When his boat arrived back in New York, Charles Rector and Diamond Jim were waiting anxiously at the pier. Before the boat had even docked, Brady shouted up to young Rector, "Have you got the sauce?"

The three men quickly drove to Charles Rector's. That night Diamond Jim fully indulged himself. He polished off nine plates of fish smothered in the sauce. Satisfied at last, he turned to Charles Rector and said, "If you poured some of the sauce over a Turkish towel, I believe I could eat all of it."

Diamond Jim's eating habits finally caught up with him. He developed serious stomach problems. His days as a fabled eater came to an end. He died in 1917 at the age of sixty-one. After his death, doctors discovered that his stomach had stretched to six times the size of a normal stomach. ■

If you have been timed while reading this selection, enter your reading time below. Then turn to the Words per Minute table on page 154 and look up your reading speed (words per minute). Enter your reading speed on the graph on page 156.

READING TIME: Unit 6
———— : ————
Minutes   *Seconds*

How well did you read?

- *Answer the four types of questions that follow. The directions for each type of question tell you how to mark your answers.*

- *When you have finished all four exercises, check your work by using the answer key on page 150. For each right answer, put a check mark (✔) on the line beside the box. For each wrong answer, write the correct answer on the line.*

- *For scoring each exercise, follow the directions below the questions.*

A FINDING THE MAIN IDEA

Look at the three statements below. One expresses the main idea of the story you just read. A good main idea statement answers two questions: it tells *who* or *what* is the subject of the story, and it answers the understood question *does what?* or *is what?* Another statement is *too broad,* it is vague and doesn't tell much about the topic of the story. The third statement is *too narrow,* it tells about only one part of the story.

Match the statements with the three answer choices below by writing the letter of each answer in the box in front of the statement it goes with.

M—Main Idea   B—Too Broad   N—Too Narrow

____ ☐ 1. Diamond Jim Brady had a great love for diamonds and an even greater love for food.

____ ☐ 2. Diamond Jim Brady was a nineteenth-century millionaire who lived in New York City.

____ ☐ 3. Diamond Jim Brady lived a life of excess.

____ Score 15 points for a correct *M* answer

____ Score 5 points for each correct *B* or *N* answer

____ TOTAL SCORE: Finding the Main Idea

B RECALLING FACTS

How well do you remember the facts in the story you just read? Put an *x* in the box in front of the correct answer to each of the multiple choice questions below.

1. Jim Brady made his fortune by
   - ___ ☐ a. owning and running fine restaurants.
   - ___ ☐ b. selling railroad equipment.
   - ___ ☐ c. running a saloon.

2. Diamond Jim never drank
   - ___ ☐ a. milk.
   - ___ ☐ b. orange juice.
   - ___ ☐ c. alcohol.

3. Charles Rector's son went to Paris to
   - ___ ☐ a. steal the recipe for a special fish sauce.
   - ___ ☐ b. open a candy store.
   - ___ ☐ c. buy rare French coffee beans.

4. The St. James Hotel refused to let Brady
   - ___ ☐ a. eat at the employees' free lunch bar.
   - ___ ☐ b. pay for the meals he ate there.
   - ___ ☐ c. wear his diamond rings in the dining room.

5. After Brady's death, doctors learned that his stomach had
   - ___ ☐ a. been filled with cancer.
   - ___ ☐ b. stretched to six times its normal size.
   - ___ ☐ c. a tapeworm in it.

Score 5 points for each correct answer

___ TOTAL SCORE: Recalling Facts

C MAKING INFERENCES

An inference is a judgment that is made or an idea that is arrived at based on facts or on information that is given. You make an inference when you understand something that is *not* stated directly, but that is *implied*, or suggested by the facts that are given.

Below are five statements that are judgments or ideas that have been arrived at from the facts of the story. Write the letter *C* in the box in front of each statement that is a correct inference. Write the letter *F* in front of each faulty inference.

C—Correct Inference   F—Faulty Inference

- ___ ☐ 1. Though Jim Brady ate a lot, he ate a balanced diet.
- ___ ☐ 2. Jim Brady worried constantly about his health.
- ___ ☐ 3. Jim Brady found great wealth impressive.
- ___ ☐ 4. Diamond Jim spent a lot of money in Charles Rector's restaurant.
- ___ ☐ 5. By the time of his death, Jim Brady had no money left.

Score 5 points for each correct answer

___ TOTAL SCORE: Making Inferences

D USING WORDS PRECISELY

Each of the numbered sentences below contains an underlined word or phrase from the story you have just read. Under the sentence are three definitions. One has the *same* meaning as the underlined word or phrase, one has *almost the same* meaning, and one has the *opposite* meaning. Match the definitions with the three answer choices by writing the letter that stands for each answer in the box in front of the definition it goes with.

S—Same   A—Almost the Same   O—Opposite

1. Before reaching the age of thirty, he had <u>amassed</u> a sizable fortune.

____ ☐ a. used up

____ ☐ b. accumulated

____ ☐ c. located

2. His appetite knew no <u>bounds</u>.

____ ☐ a. edges

____ ☐ b. beginnings

____ ☐ c. limits

3. In fact, some of his friends wondered why he didn't drop dead in the middle of one of his <u>colossal</u> meals.

____ ☐ a. great

____ ☐ b. enormous

____ ☐ c. tiny

4. Diamond Jim followed that with a tray full of pastries and his <u>customary</u> two-pound box of chocolates.

____ ☐ a. usual

____ ☐ b. rare

____ ☐ c. ordinary

5. That night Diamond Jim fully <u>indulged</u> himself.

____ ☐ a. gave in to desires

____ ☐ b. pleased

____ ☐ c. denied

____ Score 3 points for each correct S answer

____ Score 1 point for each correct A or O answer

____ TOTAL SCORE: Using Words Precisely

- *Enter the four total scores in the spaces below, and add them together to find your Critical Reading Score. Then record your Critical Reading Score on the graph on page 157.*

_____ Finding the Main Idea
_____ Recalling Facts
_____ Making Inferences
_____ Using Words Precisely

_____ CRITICAL READING SCORE: Unit 6

Sylvester Graham started life as an unhappy misfit. He always seemed to be out of step with those around him. Eventually, though, one of his unusual ideas caught on. For a while Sylvester was on top of the world—which was right where he wanted to be. He even invented several products that he named after himself. Though Sylvester Graham's notions eventually lost favor, to this day his name remains a household word.

Sylvester Graham: You Are What You Eat

Sylvester Graham wanted to be famous. He wanted to be a leader of people. He wanted to go down in history as a reformer, a trailblazer, a man with a vision. Many young men in the 1830s shared that goal. But Sylvester planned to win his fame in a most unusual way. He was going to become famous by talking about bread.

At first no one took Sylvester seriously. They thought he was kidding. That did not surprise him. He had been laughed at many times before. Earlier, as a student at Amherst College, he had served as the butt of many jokes. He had often gotten carried away with strange ideas. In fact, he was such a misfit that school officials asked him to leave. For several years after that, Sylvester felt out of place in the world. His depression finally led to a nervous breakdown. By the mid-1830s, however, Sylvester felt like a new man. He believed he had found the key to happiness. He had uncovered the cause of everyone's problems. The secret to a happy life, he believed, lay in a person's diet.

Sylvester made his discovery by accident. It happened in Philadelphia. He had made friends with a group of vegetarians. They shared with him their ideas about food. In order to live a healthy life, they said, a person had to eat healthy foods.

The truth of that notion struck Sylvester with great force. As he looked around, he saw people wallowing in unhealthy foods. It suddenly seemed to him that he had found his mission in life. He would devote himself to telling people the dangers of a bad diet.

Sylvester faced one small problem. He had to decide which foods were bad and which were good. He solved that problem simply by sitting down and drawing up a list. Any food that seemed healthy to him went on the good list. Any food that seem unhealthy went on the bad list. Armed with his new diet, Sylvester hit the lecture circuit. He began preaching about the blessings of the Graham diet.

In his speeches, Sylvester stressed one thing: bran. No one, he said, could have good health without it. He believed it to be the single most important food. Bran was present in whole wheat flour. It was missing from the processed flour used in white bread. Sylvester therefore commanded his listeners to cut white bread from their diets. He recommended instead his own special bread. It was made with what he called "Graham flour." Graham flour was a coarse, unsifted whole wheat flour with none of the bran taken out.

Sylvester did not stop there. In order for the bread to be truly beneficial, he said, it had to be made at home. It had to be baked by the wife or mother of the family. No servant could touch it. That way, the woman baking the bread would instill it with plenty of love. Furthermore, Sylvester advised people not to eat the bread until it was at least twelve hours old. Stale bread, he declared, was healthier than fresh bread. For those who did not like bread at all, Sylvester created a cracker. It contained lots of his special flour. He called it a "Graham cracker."

Sylvester advised his followers to eat plenty of fruits and vegetables. He told them to avoid coffee, tea, salt, butter, and shellfish. He also warned against meats and fat. Those foods, he cautioned, made people lose their tempers. Even more dangerous were ketchup and mustard. Sylvester believed that they drove people to insanity. He did waver when it came to forming an opinion about milk, eggs, and honey. They might be harmless, but he couldn't be sure. He advised people not to consume them in large quantities.

Some people viewed Sylvester as a lunatic. But more and more Americans began to sit up and take notice. He made people realize how many little aches and pains they felt. He convinced them that they would feel healthier if they followed his advice.

Soon Sylvester Graham had become one of the most popular speakers in the country. People across the land listened eagerly to what he had to say. They rushed to follow his advice. Soon he expanded his talks to include more than just rules for eating. He developed guidelines for a whole new life-style. Fresh air and daily exercise were key elements in his recipe for healthy living. Hard beds and cold showers also played a major role. Sylvester announced that everyone should sleep in a room with open windows, even in winter. He also proclaimed that food could be digested properly only if people smiled during meals.

By the late 1830s, special Graham hotels and boardinghouses had sprung up. They catered to "Grahamites," as Sylvester's followers called themselves. Guests had to stick to a strict daily routine. Meals consisted of Graham bread, rice, baked beans, and a weak, tasteless pudding. No other foods were allowed on the premises.

By 1840, Sylvester had achieved his goal. He had become famous, mainly by talking about bread. After a few years, though, people grew tired of his message. They lost their enthusiasm for his demanding life-style. Gradually they forgot about Sylvester Graham. Some of his ideas did survive, however. Graham crackers are still popular. And many people consider whole wheat bread healthier than white bread. But in the 1840s, the majority of Americans realized the silliness of many of Graham's ideas. By the time Sylvester Graham died in 1851, most people considered him just another nut in the fruitcake. ■

If you have been timed while reading this selection, enter your reading time below. Then turn to the Words per Minute table on page 154 and look up your reading speed (words per minute). Enter your reading speed on the graph on page 156.

READING TIME: Unit 7

_____ : _____
Minutes   *Seconds*

How well did you read?

- *Answer the four types of questions that follow. The directions for each type of question tell you how to mark your answers.*

- *When you have finished all four exercises, check your work by using the answer key on page 150. For each right answer, put a check mark (✔) on the line beside the box. For each wrong answer, write the correct answer on the line.*

- *For scoring each exercise, follow the directions below the questions.*

A FINDING THE MAIN IDEA

Look at the three statements below. One expresses the main idea of the story you just read. A good main idea statement answers two questions: it tells *who* or *what* is the subject of the story, and it answers the understood question *does what?* or *is what?* Another statement is *too broad*, it is vague and doesn't tell much about the topic of the story. The third statement is *too narrow*, it tells about only one part of the story.

Match the statements with the three answer choices below by writing the letter of each answer in the box in front of the statement it goes with.

M—Main Idea   B—Too Broad   N—Too Narrow

____ ☐ 1. Sylvester Graham became famous by promoting his own unusual diet and general health program.

____ ☐ 2. Sylvester Graham believed that bran was basic to a healthy diet.

____ ☐ 3. Sylvester Graham persuaded many people to believe in a bizarre program that he devised.

____ Score 15 points for a correct *M* answer

____ Score 5 points for each correct *B* or *N* answer

____ TOTAL SCORE: Finding the Main Idea

B RECALLING FACTS

How well do you remember the facts in the story you just read? Put an *x* in the box in front of the correct answer to each of the multiple choice questions below.

1. Sylvester believed that the secret to a happy life lay in a person's
   ____ ☐ a. attitude.
   ____ ☐ b. diet.
   ____ ☐ c. job.

2. Sylvester Graham was the creator of
   ____ ☐ a. white bread.
   ____ ☐ b. bran.
   ____ ☐ c. a flour that he named after himself.

3. Sylvester believed that ketchup and mustard caused people to
   ____ ☐ a. go blind.
   ____ ☐ b. age.
   ____ ☐ c. go insane.

4. To spread his ideas, Sylvester Graham
   ____ ☐ a. wrote books and pamphlets.
   ____ ☐ b. gave lectures.
   ____ ☐ c. set up schools.

5. At Grahamite hotels, people ate
   ____ ☐ a. Graham bread and baked beans.
   ____ ☐ b. only bread baked by married women.
   ____ ☐ c. seafood and bread.

Score 5 points for each correct answer

____ TOTAL SCORE: Recalling Facts

C MAKING INFERENCES

An inference is a judgment that is made or an idea that is arrived at based on facts or on information that is given. You make an inference when you understand something that is *not* stated directly, but that is *implied,* or suggested by the facts that are given.

Below are five statements that are judgments or ideas that have been arrived at from the facts of the story. Write the letter *C* in the box in front of each statement that is a correct inference. Write the letter *F* in front of each faulty inference.

C—Correct Inference   F—Faulty Inference

____ ☐ 1. Sylvester was not very happy in college.

____ ☐ 2. Sylvester Graham had a degree in medicine.

____ ☐ 3. Sylvester Graham's program forms the basis for many health club programs today.

____ ☐ 4. All Graham hotels were owned by Sylvester Graham.

____ ☐ 5. Graham became popular mainly because people were eager for some kind of program that would make them feel healthier.

Score 5 points for each correct answer

____ TOTAL SCORE: Making Inferences

D USING WORDS PRECISELY

Each of the numbered sentences below contains an underlined word or phrase from the story you have just read. Under the sentence are three definitions. One has the *same* meaning as the underlined word or phrase, one has *almost the same* meaning, and one has the *opposite* meaning. Match the definitions with the three answer choices by writing the letter that stands for each answer in the box in front of the definition it goes with.

S—Same   A—Almost the Same   O—Opposite

1. Earlier, as a student at Amherst College, he had served as the underlined butt of many jokes.

____ ☐ a. receiver

____ ☐ b. creator

____ ☐ c. victim

2. He began preaching about the blessings of the Graham diet.

____ ☐ a. benefits

____ ☐ b. drawbacks

____ ☐ c. qualities

3. That way, the woman baking the bread would instill it with plenty of love.

____ ☐ a. pack

____ ☐ b. put in

____ ☐ c. removed from

4. He did waver when it came to forming an opinion about milk, eggs, and honey.

____ ☐ a. decide firmly

____ ☐ b. hesitate

____ ☐ c. change his mind

5. Hard beds and cold showers also played a prominent role.

____ ☐ a. important

____ ☐ b. real

____ ☐ c. minor

____ Score 3 points for each correct *S* answer
____ Score 1 point for each correct *A* or *O* answer

____ TOTAL SCORE: Using Words Precisely

● *Enter the four total scores in the spaces below, and add them together to find your Critical Reading Score. Then record your Critical Reading Score on the graph on page 157.*

_____	Finding the Main Idea
_____	Recalling Facts
_____	Making Inferences
_____	Using Words Precisely
_____	**CRITICAL READING SCORE: Unit 7**

GROUP TWO

There was nothing about his appearance
that would make people suspicious. He
didn't strike one as being mischievous or
difficult. But only the unexpected could
be expected from Hugh Troy. Many an
unsuspecting person was left shaking his
head—or his fist—over Troy's shenanigans.
Perhaps Troy's art, which earned him
his living, provides a glimpse into the
man's unusual mind. Here he sits in front
of a mural he painted for a restaurant.

Hugh Troy: Just Joking

The zoologists couldn't believe their eyes, but the evidence was clear. The tracks in the snow definitely belonged to a rhinoceros. They led across the campus of Cornell University, in New York, and out onto a frozen lake. Fifty feet from the shore, the tracks ended at a great gaping hole. It appeared that the rhino had fallen through the thin ice and drowned.

Local newspapers picked up the story. A group of citizens planned to dredge the lake for the animal as soon as the ice melted. Since the lake was the source of Cornell's drinking water, many people on campus refused to drink tap water. Those who did drink it swore that they could taste the rhino in it.

After several days' worth of laughs, Hugh Troy began spreading the word that the whole thing was a joke—a giant hoax. Of course, he didn't identify himself as the guilty party. The students and teachers might have thrown him into the icy lake to join his phony rhino.

Hugh Troy was an art student at Cornell, and he loved to play practical jokes. He thought up the rhino prank one day when he spotted a friend's wastepaper basket, which was made from a rhinoceros foot. Hugh borrowed the wastepaper basket and filled it with scrap metal to give it weight. He then attached a long rope to each side. All he needed after that was a few inches of snow.

Late one night the snow finally fell. Hugh and a friend sneaked out onto the deserted campus with the rhino foot. They each took hold of one of the ropes and moved as far apart as they could, with the weighted rhinoceros foot suspended between them. Then they walked slowly across the campus, carefully raising and lowering the foot in the snow at the proper intervals to make believable rhinoceros tracks. Hugh and his friend then sat back and waited for the fun to begin.

After his days at Cornell, Hugh Troy became a successful artist and writer. From the 1930s until his death in 1964, he created murals that brightened the walls of some of the most famous buildings in the United States. He also wrote and illustrated children's books. But in his spare time he still looked for opportunities to play tricks on people. He specialized in outrageous and sometimes risky pranks. He wanted to put a little excitement into his own and other people's lives. Life without a few harmless tricks, Hugh thought, could be pretty drab.

While living in New York City, Hugh spiced up his life at the expense of the police. One day he decided to dig a hole eight feet wide and five feet deep in the middle of Fifth Avenue. Naturally, he had no right to do that. He just wanted to see if he could get away with it. So he and several friends posed as construction workers. They wore old overalls and set out "Men Working" signs. Then, with picks and shovels, they began ripping up the pavement.

It all looked so official that the police never asked what they were doing. It wasn't until the next day that the police realized what had happened. By then, of course, Hugh and his merry men were long gone and nowhere to be found. The police did not discover who was responsible until many years later.

Hugh, however, was not through with the New York City police. One day he bought a park bench identical to the benches in Central Park. He and a friend sneaked into the park with the bench, sat down, and waited. As soon as a police officer came within view, Hugh and his friend picked up the bench and started walking away with it. The officer immediately arrested them, of course.

In court Hugh produced his sales receipt for the bench. A person cannot, after all, steal his own park bench. After being found not guilty, Hugh pretended to be deeply hurt. He lectured the judge on false arrest and the rights of the individual.

When he left the courthouse, he enjoyed a good laugh. But he was not content to leave the joke at that. He proceeded to repeat the same stunt several times. Each time, he was arrested by a different police officer, and each time the judge released him when he produced the receipt for the purchase. Hugh quit only when word of his joke had spread among the angry park police. He knew they were tired of being made fools of, and that he wouldn't get away with the prank again.

In 1935 Hugh pulled off one of his greatest hoaxes. The Museum of Modern Art in New York City was planning its first showing of the works of Vincent Van Gogh. Most people, however, seemed more interested in the artist's unusual personal life than in his paintings. In particular, they wanted to know more about why Van Gogh had cut off one of his own ears. When the show opened, visitors flooded the museum. Hugh felt that most people were going because they were fascinated by scandal, not because they loved art. He decided to prove his point by separating the true art lover from the thrill-seeker.

Hugh took a piece of dried beef and molded it into the likeness of a withered human ear. He then mounted the "ear" in a blue velvet box. Somehow he managed to smuggle the phony ear into the museum. He placed it on a table near the Van Gogh paintings. Under the box he put a neatly-lettered sign that read: This is the ear Vincent Van Gogh cut off, Dec. 24, 1888. Hugh understood human nature pretty well. Most of the visitors flocked around what they believed was Vincent Van Gogh's severed ear, leaving the true art enthusiasts plenty of room to view Van Gogh's paintings.

During World War II, Hugh took on the United States Army. As a young officer, he was required to fill out countless reports. Every little detail needed a report, it seemed. Soon Hugh rebelled against all that paperwork. He decided to do something that would make a statement about just how silly and useless all that paperwork was.

In the mess hall, where the soldiers ate, flypaper ribbons hung from the ceiling. Hugh drafted his own report detailing the number of flies that were caught by each strip of flypaper. He identified each strip by a code number. Hugh made his bogus report as complicated as possible. Each day he included a flypaper report with all the other reports he sent to Washington.

Before long two of Hugh's fellow officers paid him a visit. Officials in Washington wanted to know why they hadn't been filing *their* flypaper reports. Had Hugh heard anything about a flypaper report? Of course he had, he told the two officers. He gave them copies of his report so that they could start filing their own. Word spread throughout the post, and soon every officer was filing a flypaper report.

No one knows what Washington did with all those reports. The only thing we know for sure is that Hugh Troy, the tireless practical joker, had more than his fair share of laughs. ■

If you have been timed while reading this selection, enter your reading time below. Then turn to the Words per Minute table on page 155 and look up your reading speed (words per minute). Enter your reading speed on the graph on page 156.

READING TIME: Unit 8

—————— : ——————
Minutes   *Seconds*

How well did you read?

- *Answer the four types of questions that follow. The directions for each type of question tell you how to mark your answers.*

- *When you have finished all four exercises, check your work by using the answer key on page 151. For each right answer, put a check mark (✓) on the line beside the box. For each wrong answer, write the correct answer on the line.*

- *For scoring each exercise, follow the directions below the questions.*

A FINDING THE MAIN IDEA

Look at the three statements below. One expresses the main idea of the story you just read. A good main idea statement answers two questions: it tells *who* or *what* is the subject of the story, and it answers the understood question *does what?* or *is what?* Another statement is *too broad,* it is vague and doesn't tell much about the topic of the story. The third statement is *too narrow,* it tells about only one part of the story.

Match the statements with the three answer choices below by writing the letter of each answer in the box in front of the statement it goes with.

M—Main Idea   **B—Too Broad**   **N—Too Narrow**

____ ☐ 1. Hugh Troy set up a phony exhibit of Vincent Van Gogh's ear in New York's Museum of Modern Art.

____ ☐ 2. Hugh Troy wanted to put excitement into his own life and into the lives of others.

____ ☐ 3. Hugh Troy was a great practical joker.

____ Score 15 points for a correct *M* answer

____ Score 5 points for each correct *B* or *N* answer

____ TOTAL SCORE: Finding the Main Idea

B RECALLING FACTS

How well do you remember the facts in the story you just read?
Put an x in the box in front of the correct answer to each of the multiple choice questions below.

1. While a student at Cornell University, Hugh Troy pressed a wastebasket into the snow to make footprints of a
____ ☐ a. hippopotamus.
____ ☐ b. rhinoceros.
____ ☐ c. water buffalo.

2. Hugh Troy dug a hole in the middle of Fifth Avenue because
____ ☐ a. a judge ordered him to work on a construction project.
____ ☐ b. army officers dared him to do it.
____ ☐ c. he wanted to see if he could get away with it.

3. At one point, police officers kept arresting Hugh Troy because they thought Troy was trying to steal a
____ ☐ a. "Men Working" sign.
____ ☐ b. park bench.
____ ☐ c. painting from the Museum of Modern Art.

4. To make a fake ear that he claimed was Vincent Van Gogh's, Hugh Troy used
____ ☐ a. clay.
____ ☐ b. dried beef.
____ ☐ c. plaster of paris.

5. While in the army, Hugh Troy confused officials by writing reports about
____ ☐ a. flypaper.
____ ☐ b. the number of soldiers eating in the mess hall.
____ ☐ c. officers' code names.

Score 5 points for each correct answer

____ TOTAL SCORE: Recalling Facts

C MAKING INFERENCES

An inference is a judgment that is made or an idea that is arrived at based on facts or on information that is given. You make an inference when you understand something that is *not* stated directly, but that is *implied*, or suggested by the facts that are given.

Below are five statements that are judgments or ideas that have been arrived at from the facts of the story. Write the letter *C* in the box in front of each statement that is a correct inference. Write the letter *F* in front of each faulty inference.

C—Correct Inference   F—Faulty Inference

____ ☐ 1. Many people at Cornell were angry about being fooled by the rhino hoax.

____ ☐ 2. Hugh Troy was a respected artist.

____ ☐ 3. No one was fooled by the phony Vincent Van Gogh ear.

____ ☐ 4. Hugh Troy particularly enjoyed practical jokes aimed at people in authority.

____ ☐ 5. All army reports are as useless as Hugh Troy's flypaper reports.

Score 5 points for each correct answer

____ TOTAL SCORE: Making Inferences

D USING WORDS PRECISELY

Each of the numbered sentences below contains an underlined word or phrase from the story you have just read. Under the sentence are three definitions. One has the *same* meaning as the underlined word or phrase, one has *almost the same* meaning, and one has the *opposite* meaning. Match the definitions with the three answer choices by writing the letter that stands for each answer in the box in front of the definition it goes with.

S—Same   A—Almost the Same   O—Opposite

1. After several days' worth of laughs, Hugh Troy began spreading the word that the whole thing was a joke—a giant <u>hoax</u>.

____ ☐ a. fact

____ ☐ b. game

____ ☐ c. scam

2. They each took hold of one of the ropes and moved as far apart as they could, with the weighted rhinoceros foot <u>suspended</u> between them.

____ ☐ a. hanging

____ ☐ b. dragging

____ ☐ c. held up

3. Hugh felt that most people were going because they were fascinated by <u>scandal</u>, not because they loved art.

____ ☐ a. outrageous incidents

____ ☐ b. shocking incidents

____ ☐ c. respectable incidents

4. Most of the visitors flocked around what they believed was Vincent Van Gogh's <u>severed</u> ear.

____ ☐ a. damaged

____ ☐ b. attached

____ ☐ c. cut off

5. Hugh made his <u>bogus</u> report as complicated as possible.

____ ☐ a. phony

____ ☐ b. ridiculous

____ ☐ c. actual

____ Score 3 points for each correct *S* answer
____ Score 1 point for each correct *A* or *O* answer

____ **TOTAL SCORE:** Using Words Precisely

● *Enter the four total scores in the spaces below, and add them together to find your Critical Reading Score. Then record your Critical Reading Score on the graph on page 157.*

_____ Finding the Main Idea
_____ Recalling Facts
_____ Making Inferences
_____ Using Words Precisely
_____ **CRITICAL READING SCORE:** Unit 8

What in the world? John Cleves Symmes's answer to that question would have been "Another world." You see, Symmes had some definite, if unusual, theories about what goes on inside our planet. In his view, the inside of the earth was an active place indeed. He was excited about his ideas, and wanted nothing more than a chance to prove them correct. For that, he needed support, and he set out to get it. Most people laughed at him. But Symmes was such a persuasive man that he was able to convince some powerful people that his theories were worth investigating.

John Cleves Symmes and the Hollow Earth

The people on the inside of the earth don't have to worry about getting sunburned. They live where the sun doesn't shine. Still, theirs is not a land of total darkness. Some sunlight is reflected into their towns and villages through two giant holes in the earth's surface. The hole at the North Pole measures four thousand miles across. An even larger hole at the South Pole spans six thousand miles.

That was part of the earth theory of Captain John Cleves Symmes, a military hero of the War of 1812. Symmes was an amateur scientist who read every science book available. He also studied the planets through his telescope. His studies convinced him that the earth was hollow. But he was equally sure it wasn't empty.

As Symmes saw it, the hollow earth contained another, smaller planet. And inside that smaller planet was still another planet, and so on. Each of the interior planets had huge openings at its poles. In all, five planets existed inside the earth. The whole was like a child's toy, each ball fitting neatly into a larger ball. Supposedly, people lived and worked in each of the smaller worlds.

While other explorers of the day were investigating the Rocky Mountains, Antarctica, and other little-known places on the earth, Symmes set his sights on a far more ambitious expedition. He wanted to open up whole new worlds for exploration and discovery—worlds within our own.

Symmes was not the first person to imagine that the earth might be hollow. Over two thousand years ago, the Greek philosopher Plato suggested that possibility. A famous nineteenth-century Scottish scientist named Sir John Lesley believed that the earth was hollow and that it contained two small suns. Dr. Edmund Halley, after whom the famous comet was named, also thought the earth was hollow. In fact, Halley believed that three planets the sizes of Venus, Mars, and Mercury revolved inside the earth.

But Symmes went much further than any of those thinkers. Not only were his theories more elaborate, but he wanted to confirm their validity, as well. He actually wanted to travel to the inside of the earth. He planned to go to the North Pole with a hundred other valiant souls and travel through the giant hole to the earth's interior.

However, as Symmes saw it, that was not simply a matter of jumping into a huge hole and hoping for the best. Rather, one would just keep heading north until one started walking downhill and, finally, upside down. The earth's surface gradually curved in on itself. So a traveler could be at the rim of the hole and not even know it. He or she would slowly enter the interior and finally end up on the inside surface of the earth's crust. The traveler would not, however, tumble off the inside of the shell. Symmes dismissed the common notion of gravity. He believed that the air contained an invisible fluid that kept people safely pressed to the earth's surface. To Symmes, people on the inside of the earth could walk around as easily as people in Australia, who, in a sense, live upside down on the bottom of the world.

Of course, exploring the inside of the earth's crust would take money. And Symmes didn't have any. So he needed to convert people to his cause. He mailed bulletins about his theories to prominent scientists and politicians around the world. With each notice, Symmes included a doctor's note testifying to his sanity. Most people politely ignored his bulletin. But he did manage to persuade some important people. For instance, he won the support of Richard M. Johnson, a member of Congress from Kentucky, and future vice president of the United States. Johnson asked the House of Representatives to fund an expedition led by Symmes. The House flatly refused.

The idea, however, did not die. Symmes

would not let it. Again he worked hard to rally public support. He spoke to large audiences attracted by his novel ideas. He wrote dozens of newspaper and magazine articles. Most importantly, he got hundreds of people to sign a petition. In January of 1823, Representative Johnson presented the petition to the House. It demanded that Congress vote the funds Symmes needed. After all, exploring the inside of the earth promised great things. Who could say what new people might be found? Or what new lands could be explored? Or what new and profitable trade routes might be opened?

The House was unsure of what to do. Most members thought the idea was ludicrous. But Symmes *was* a war hero and some respectable people *had* signed the petition. So the House decided to do nothing. They just let the petition sit there. That only produced a flood of additional petitions. Clearly, some people were excited by Symmes's scheme. Finally goaded into action, the House voted the project down for the second time. Still, there were twenty-five votes in favor of the project.

Where others saw defeat, Symmes saw victory. The twenty-five "yes" votes inspired him. He dedicated the rest of his life to proving his theories correct. For the next few years, Symmes toured the country. People still flocked to see him, but now they went mostly out of curiosity. They loved to hear him describe "Symmes's Hole," but they were less enthusiastic about donating money for his planned expedition. Symmes couldn't raise enough money to get the expedition going.

Then, in 1825, it looked as though he was at last going to get the break he needed. The Russian government began preparing to explore the regions near the North Pole. Symmes offered his services on the expedition. He impressed the Russians with his knowledge of the arctic regions. In fact, the Russian leaders believed in Symmes's theory about a hollow earth. So they accepted his offer of help. Unfortunately for Symmes, however, he wasn't able to raise enough money to pay his fare to Russia.

So the Russians went without him. Poor Symmes could only wait helplessly for word of their discoveries. When that word finally came, it was disheartening. The Russians had found plenty of ice and snow. They had found a few polar bears. But they hadn't found a single hole leading to the inside of the earth.

That put Symmes back where he had started. Still, he refused to alter his theory. He remained convinced that his vision was correct. He continued to deliver passionate lectures on the subject, and to write articles for newspapers and magazines.

In 1828, Symmes fell ill and never recovered. On May 29, 1829, Captain John Cleves Symmes died at the age of forty-nine. His theory survived him, at least for a time. There were people who clung to the idea of a hollow earth for many more years. But eventually even the theory died. When explorers reached the North and South Poles in the twentieth century, they proved once and for all that Symmes's Hole did not exist. ■

If you have been timed while reading this selection, enter your reading time below. Then turn to the Words per Minute table on page 155 and look up your reading speed (words per minute). Enter your reading speed on the graph on page 156.

READING TIME: Unit 9

_____ : _____
Minutes   *Seconds*

How well did you read?

- *Answer the four types of questions that follow. The directions for each type of question tell you how to mark your answers.*

- *When you have finished all four exercises, check your work by using the answer key on page 151. For each right answer, put a check mark (✓) on the line beside the box. For each wrong answer, write the correct answer on the line.*

- *For scoring each exercise, follow the directions below the questions.*

A FINDING THE MAIN IDEA

Look at the three statements below. One expresses the main idea of the story you just read. A good main idea statement answers two questions: it tells *who* or *what* is the subject of the story, and it answers the understood question *does what?* or *is what?* Another statement is *too broad*, it is vague and doesn't tell much about the topic of the story. The third statement is *too narrow*, it tells about only one part of the story.

Match the statements with the three answer choices below by writing the letter of each answer in the box in front of the statement it goes with.

M—Main Idea   **B—Too Broad**   **N—Too Narrow**

____ ☐ 1. John Cleves Symmes wanted to explore the area around the North Pole.

____ ☐ 2. John Cleves Symmes was fascinated by theories about the structure of the earth.

____ ☐ 3. John Cleves Symmes spent much of his life trying to prove that the earth was hollow.

____ Score 15 points for a correct *M* answer

____ Score 5 points for each correct *B* or *N* answer

____ TOTAL SCORE: Finding the Main Idea

B RECALLING FACTS

How well do you remember the facts in the story you just read? Put an *x* in the box in front of the correct answer to each of the multiple choice questions below.

1. John Cleves Symmes believed that inside the earth there existed
   ____ ☐ a. three smaller planets.
   ____ ☐ b. five smaller planets.
   ____ ☐ c. ten smaller planets.

2. Symmes did not believe in the common theory of
   ____ ☐ a. relativity.
   ____ ☐ b. gravity.
   ____ ☐ c. evolution.

3. Richard M. Johnson wanted the House of Representatives to give Symmes money for
   ____ ☐ a. an expedition to the North Pole.
   ____ ☐ b. a trip to Russia.
   ____ ☐ c. a visit to Australia.

4. When Symmes mailed bulletins to prominent people asking for their support, he included
   ____ ☐ a. a statement of support from Sir John Lesley.
   ____ ☐ b. a map showing the route to the earth's interior.
   ____ ☐ c. a doctor's note declaring him sane.

5. When the Russians explored the North Pole, they found
   ____ ☐ a. a small hole leading deep into the earth.
   ____ ☐ b. ice, snow, and a few polar bears.
   ____ ☐ c. debris from Halley's Comet.

Score 5 points for each correct answer

____ TOTAL SCORE: Recalling Facts

C MAKING INFERENCES

An inference is a judgment that is made or an idea that is arrived at based on facts or on information that is given. You make an inference when you understand something that is *not* stated directly, but that is *implied*, or suggested by the facts that are given.

Below are five statements that are judgments or ideas that have been arrived at from the facts of the story. Write the letter *C* in the box in front of each statement that is a correct inference. Write the letter *F* in front of each faulty inference.

C—Correct Inference   F—Faulty Inference

____ ☐ 1. In 1825, no one knew that Mars existed.

____ ☐ 2. Symmes feared that many people thought he was insane.

____ ☐ 3. In the Arctic, the Russians did not look very hard for a hole leading into the earth.

____ ☐ 4. "Symmes's Hole" was the name given to the hole Symmes believed existed at the North Pole.

____ ☐ 5. Symmes read a great deal of science fiction.

Score 5 points for each correct answer

____ TOTAL SCORE: Making Inferences

D USING WORDS PRECISELY

Each of the numbered sentences below contains an underlined word or phrase from the story you have just read. Under the sentence are three definitions. One has the *same* meaning as the underlined word or phrase, one has *almost the same* meaning, and one has the *opposite* meaning. Match the definitions with the three answer choices by writing the letter that stands for each answer in the box in front of the definition it goes with.

S—Same   A—Almost the Same   O—Opposite

1. Symmes <u>dismissed</u> the common notion of gravity.

___ ☐ a. embraced

___ ☐ b. rejected

___ ☐ c. disliked

2. He planned to go to the North Pole with a hundred other <u>valiant</u> souls and travel through the giant hole to the earth's interior.

___ ☐ a. cowardly

___ ☐ b. courageous

___ ☐ c. adventuresome

3. Most members thought the idea was <u>ludicrous</u>.

___ ☐ a. absurd

___ ☐ b. amusing

___ ☐ c. sensible

4. Finally <u>goaded</u> into action, the House voted the project down for the second time.

___ ☐ a. prodded

___ ☐ b. forced

___ ☐ c. held back

5. When that word finally came, it was <u>disheartening</u>.

___ ☐ a. discouraging

___ ☐ b. encouraging

___ ☐ c. upsetting

___ Score 3 points for each correct S answer
___ Score 1 point for each correct A or O answer
___ TOTAL SCORE: Using Words Precisely

● *Enter the four total scores in the spaces below, and add them together to find your Critical Reading Score. Then record your Critical Reading Score on the graph on page 157.*

_____ Finding the Main Idea
_____ Recalling Facts
_____ Making Inferences
_____ Using Words Precisely
_____ **CRITICAL READING SCORE: Unit 9**

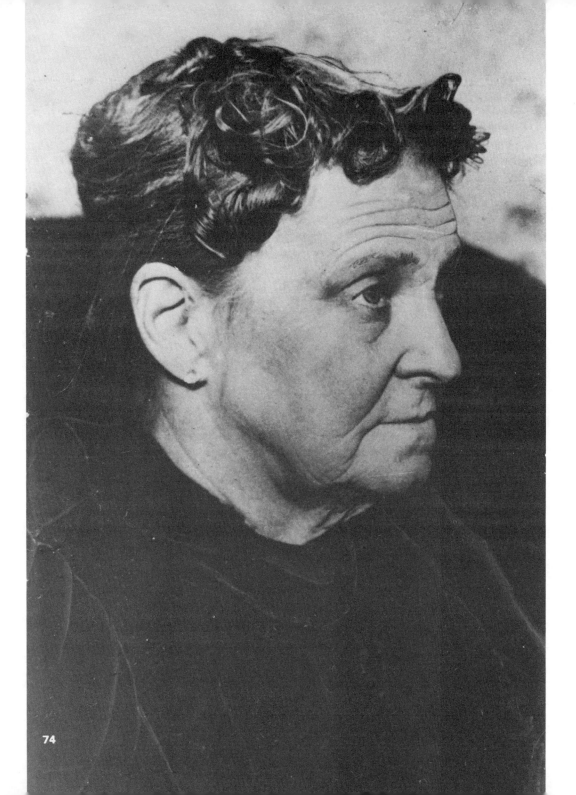

Bossy, spiteful, petty, hard, stingy, and immensely wealthy, Hetty Green lived in a way that no one who knew her, or knew about her, could understand. Some of the things she did were not only strange, but appalling. Her own son was the pathetic victim of one of her most outrageous acts.

Hetty Green: Money Was Everything

When Hetty Green walked through the streets of New York City in the 1880s, people stopped and stared. She wore ragged old black dresses. Her filthy hair lay matted against her head. Her hands and fingernails were encrusted with layers of dirt. She sometimes carried a tattered old handbag or a broken-down umbrella. In short, she looked like one of the most desperately poor residents of the city. But hidden in the pockets of her grimy clothes was thousands of dollars in cash and bonds. And that was only the beginning of her wealth. In fact, Hetty Green was the richest woman in the United States.

Hetty inherited over $1 million from her father in 1865. She inherited another million that same year from her aunt. She used her inheritance to invest in a variety of industries. Sensing that railroads were the wave of the future, she invested heavily in them. That kind of solid business sense helped her increase her fortune. By 1900, when the average American was earning $490 per year, Hetty Green's income was $7 million. Her total worth was well over $100 million.

Despite her wealth, Hetty hated the thought of spending money on clothes. In fact, the thought of spending money on *anything* made her shudder. She seldom took baths because it cost a few cents to heat bath water and a few cents more to buy soap. She refused to buy a winter coat, and instead lined her clothes with newspapers to stay warm. She even carried sandwiches in her pockets so she would never have to pay restaurant prices.

In 1867 Hetty married a millionaire named Edward Green. What they saw in each other is hard to imagine, for they didn't share the same values. Mr. Green was a gentle, generous man who loved to travel.

In 1868 the Greens had a son, Edward, whom they called Ned. Three years later they had a daughter, Sylvia. The Greens never agreed on how to raise the children. Mr. Green tended to treat them kindly and buy them presents. Hetty maintained that such treatment would only spoil them. The Greens also argued about investments. Hetty never trusted her husband with money, and kept her entire fortune in accounts separate from his. As it turned out, that proved wise. In 1873 the stock market crashed, and Edward Green lost most of his money.

Shortly after that, the couple broke up. The children stayed with their mother. Hetty did not consider changing her stingy ways for the sake of her children. She continued to amaze everyone with her tightfisted, penny-pinching habits. Once, for example, she misplaced a two-cent postage stamp while riding in a carriage. At the end of her journey, she refused to let the carriage leave until she found the stamp. She scoured the inside of that carriage for hours. Finally, in the middle of the night, she emerged from the carriage holding the stamp triumphantly in her hand.

On another occasion, she spent an entire morning rummaging through an old barn. She suspected that the barn contained things of value. When she discovered a battered sled, she knew she'd been right. The sled was in terrible condition, but it was held together by "some perfectly good nails." Hetty spent the next several hours pulling the nails out by hand. She then had a few good nails to use if she ever needed them.

Hetty went out of her way to save money on housing, too. Though she owned many valuable buildings, she rented them all out to others. She insisted that she and her family didn't need fancy houses. The Greens lived in a series of cheap, bug-ridden boarding houses. Often they had only one or two rooms. Naturally, Hetty thought that an icebox was a foolish luxury, as well, so their food often spoiled before it could be eaten.

The Greens did keep a country home in

Bellows Falls, Vermont. But in 1906 the town raised the taxes on that property. Hetty promptly boarded the place up and rarely visited it again. That didn't lower the taxes, but it did make Hetty feel good to spite the town officials.

At one point she rented a wretched little apartment in Hoboken, New Jersey. Soon, though, city officials notified her that her dog, Dewey, needed a license. The fee for a dog license was two dollars. Rather than pay that sum, Hetty moved out of New Jersey.

Hetty's stingy habits often hurt no one. But in one instance her refusal to spend money had terrible consequences. In the 1870s her young son, Ned, injured his knee while sledding. Hetty could see that the leg was in bad shape, but she refused to take Ned to a doctor. After all, doctors charged fees for their work. So Hetty kept Ned at home and hoped the leg would heal itself. She tried the home remedy of wrapping the leg in tobacco leaves. That, of course, had no effect. The leg simply grew more and more painful. Ned began limping badly. He could no longer run or jump or play games with the other children. He lived in constant pain.

Finally, in 1886, his mother decided to seek help from a doctor. But she still didn't want to spend so much as a nickel to help her son. So she turned to the free clinics. She dressed Ned in his worst rags and pretended to be a beggar. Then she went from one clinic to the next, hoping to fool a doctor into providing free treatment. Unfortunately for Ned, the Greens were fairly famous by that time. Everywhere they went, doctors and nurses recognized them. At last Hetty gave up trying. She let Ned go on suffering for another two years.

Then, in 1888, the boy collapsed on a staircase while visiting his father. Mr. Green grew furious when he learned that Ned's leg had never received any medical attention. He immediately called in his own doctor. When the doctor saw the leg, he shook his head sadly. The tissue in the leg had decayed. The whole leg would have to be amputated. "It's too bad something wasn't done sooner," the doctor said. "Five years ago we could have saved the whole limb."

Rather than risk his wife's fury at having to pay a medical bill, Mr. Green scraped together the five thousand dollars for the operation himself. A surgeon cut off Ned's leg seven inches above the knee, then fitted him with a cork leg. For the rest of his life, Ned's artificial limb served as a reminder of his mother's bizarre values.

Hetty Green lived to be eighty years old. When she died in 1916, her body was taken to Bellows Falls, Vermont. There she received a simple burial in the cemetery of the Immanuel Episcopal Church. That surprised many people. They couldn't understand why she had chosen to be buried there. Everyone knew that Hetty Green had been raised a Quaker, not an Episcopalian, and that she had quarreled with the town over taxes. One shrewd Vermonter, however, had a simple explanation for Hetty's choice of the Immanuel graveyard. "There was free space for Hetty there," he explained. ∎

If you have been timed while reading this selection, enter your reading time below. Then turn to the Words per Minute table on page 155 and look up your reading speed (words per minute). Enter your reading speed on the graph on page 156.

READING TIME: Unit 10

_____ : _____
Minutes   *Seconds*

How well did you read?

- *Answer the four types of questions that follow. The directions for each type of question tell you how to mark your answers.*

- *When you have finished all four exercises, check your work by using the answer key on page 151. For each right answer, put a check mark (✔) on the line beside the box. For each wrong answer, write the correct answer on the line.*

- *For scoring each exercise, follow the directions below the questions.*

A FINDING THE MAIN IDEA

Look at the three statements below. One expresses the main idea of the story you just read. A good main idea statement answers two questions: it tells *who* or *what* is the subject of the story, and it answers the understood question *does what?* or *is what?* Another statement is *too broad*, it is vague and doesn't tell much about the topic of the story. The third statement is *too narrow*, it tells about only one part of the story.

Match the statements with the three answer choices below by writing the letter of each answer in the box in front of the statement it goes with.

M—Main Idea   **B—Too Broad**   **N—Too Narrow**

____ ☐ 1. Although Hetty Green was the richest woman in America, she was extremely stingy.

____ ☐ 2. Hetty Green waited so long to get medical treatment for her son's injured leg that it had to be cut off.

____ ☐ 3. Hetty Green was an odd wealthy woman.

____ Score 15 points for a correct *M* answer

____ Score 5 points for each correct *B* or *N* answer

____ TOTAL SCORE: Finding the Main Idea

B RECALLING FACTS

How well do you remember the facts in the story you just read?
Put an *x* in the box in front of the correct answer to each of the
multiple choice questions below.

1. By 1900 Hetty Green's wealth totaled
   - [ ] a. $10 million.
   - [ ] b. $100 million.
   - [ ] c. $10 billion.

2. Hetty seldom took baths because she
   - [ ] a. didn't like to be clean.
   - [ ] b. hated to spend money for soap and hot water.
   - [ ] c. was afraid she would catch a cold.

3. When the town of Bellows Falls, Vermont, raised her property taxes, Hetty promptly
   - [ ] a. boarded up her house and rarely went there again.
   - [ ] b. burned her house down.
   - [ ] c. filed a lawsuit against the town.

4. Hetty's son, Ned, injured his knee while
   - [ ] a. playing football.
   - [ ] b. sledding.
   - [ ] c. pulling nails out of an old sled.

5. When Hetty took her son to free clinics, she pretended to be a
   - [ ] a. foreigner.
   - [ ] b. doctor.
   - [ ] c. beggar.

Score 5 points for each correct answer

____ TOTAL SCORE: Recalling Facts

C MAKING INFERENCES

An inference is a judgment that is made or an idea that is
arrived at based on facts or on information that is given. You
make an inference when you understand something that is *not*
stated directly, but that is *implied*, or suggested by the facts that
are given.

Below are five statements that are judgments or ideas that
have been arrived at from the facts of the story. Write the letter
C in the box in front of each statement that is a correct inference. Write the letter *F* in front of each faulty inference.

C—Correct Inference   F—Faulty Inference

1. Hetty Green was admired for the way she managed her money.

2. Hetty's children had happy childhoods.

3. Ned did not complain to his father about his injured leg.

4. Hetty would have been a nicer person if she had not had so much money.

5. After Hetty's death, Sylvia and Ned squandered their mother's fortune.

Score 5 points for each correct answer

____ TOTAL SCORE: Making Inferences

78

D USING WORDS PRECISELY

Each of the numbered sentences below contains an underlined word or phrase from the story you have just read. Under the sentence are three definitions. One has the *same* meaning as the underlined word or phrase, one has *almost the same* meaning, and one has the *opposite* meaning. Match the definitions with the three answer choices by writing the letter that stands for each answer in the box in front of the definition it goes with.

S—Same   A—Almost the Same   O—Opposite

1. Hetty <u>maintained</u> that such treatment would only spoil them.

   ____ ☐ a. disagreed

   ____ ☐ b. insisted

   ____ ☐ c. decided

2. Finally, in the middle of the night, she <u>emerged</u> from the carriage holding the stamp triumphantly in her hand.

   ____ ☐ a. came out

   ____ ☐ b. exited

   ____ ☐ c. entered

3. That didn't lower the taxes, but it did make Hetty feel good to <u>spite</u> the town officials.

   ____ ☐ a. be kind to

   ____ ☐ b. annoy

   ____ ☐ c. show ill will toward

4. At one point she rented a <u>wretched</u> little apartment in Hoboken, New Jersey.

   ____ ☐ a. poor

   ____ ☐ b. miserable

   ____ ☐ c. fine

5. One <u>shrewd</u> Vermonter, however, had a simple explanation for Hetty's choice of the Immanuel graveyard.

   ____ ☐ a. clever

   ____ ☐ b. smart

   ____ ☐ c. dull

____ Score 3 points for each correct *S* answer

____ Score 1 point for each correct *A* or *O* answer

____ **TOTAL SCORE: Using Words Precisely**

- *Enter the four total scores in the spaces below, and add them together to find your Critical Reading Score. Then record your Critical Reading Score on the graph on page 157.*

   _____ Finding the Main Idea
   _____ Recalling Facts
   _____ Making Inferences
   _____ Using Words Precisely
   _____ **CRITICAL READING SCORE: Unit 10**

A lot of people dream of "being some-body," but Timothy Dexter's desire for recognition went far beyond the ordinary. He was successful—far more so than some folks thought he ought to have been—but that wasn't enough for him. He wanted fame, respect, admiration. Some of the trappings he could buy for himself, but he just couldn't seem to win the public sentiment to go along with them. He finally did come up with a couple of ways to ensure that his name would live on—even if those ways were a little strange.

Timothy Dexter's Quest for Renown

The people of Newburyport, Massachusetts, did not like Timothy Dexter. They didn't like the ridiculous oversized hats he wore. They didn't like the outrageous letters he had published in the local newspaper. Dexter's letters condemned everything from current women's fashions to his son-in-law. But most of all, the people of Newburyport didn't like the fact that Dexter was rich. Newburyport was filled with wealthy people, and most had earned their money through years and years of hard work. They didn't think a screwball like Timothy Dexter had any right to become so rich so quickly, and by such weird means.

Dexter began his career as a poor leather dresser—he had a shop where he tanned and softened leather. While still a young man, he accumulated a small fortune by making some lucky investments. Then he really went wild. In 1790 he decided to start a shipping company, which sounded perfectly respectable at first. Then people learned what it was Dexter planned to ship. He wanted to send 42,000 warming pans to the tropical islands of the West Indies. His neighbors could not believe their ears. Warming pans were used only in cold climates, to warm the sheets on winter nights. No one in the West Indies could possibly have any use for them. But

Dexter insisted on going ahead with his plan. He had dreamed of warming pans three nights in a row, he said, and that proved the wisdom of his idea. So he packed nine ships full of the pans and sent them off to the West Indies.

The people of Newburyport sat smugly back and waited. They fully expected Dexter to be bankrupted by his folly. Instead, they learned that he had sold all his warming pans in the tropics for a 79 percent profit! It seemed that his ships had arrived in the West Indies at just the right moment. Molasses-makers there were looking for a way to skim the scum off boiling molasses. They took one look at the warming pans and snapped them up to use as molasses skimmers.

Dexter later decided to send his ships on another voyage to the West Indies. Again his choice of cargo astounded the citizens of Newburyport. He announced that he was going to ship woolen mittens to the islands. Everyone predicted that he would lose a great deal of money on his absurd scheme. But once again Dexter had the last laugh. A Russian trading ship happened to be in the West Indies when Dexter's ships arrived. The Russian merchants knew the mittens would be popular in their country during the long Russian winters. They paid high prices for

the mittens, leaving Dexter with a handsome profit.

The people of Newburyport were not amused. They felt that someone as foolish as Dexter should not be rewarded for his actions. But the man seemed to be blessed with extraordinary luck. Time after time, Dexter came up with wild plans for making money. And time after time his plans worked. He shipped stray cats to a remote island and sold them as insurance against rats. He shipped tons of Virginia coal to Newcastle, England, a city that produced more than enough coal of its own. Dexter's coal sold for ten times its ordinary value, though, because his ships arrived during a coal miners' strike. Dexter even managed to make $47,000 selling English Bibles in Spanish-speaking lands.

By 1794 Dexter had as much money as the richest families in Newburyport. But he wanted something more. He felt that his newfound wealth entitled him to the respect and admiration of his peers. He published a letter in the local newspaper suggesting that he would make a wonderful emperor of the United States. When no one responded positively to that idea, he began to pester townspeople to honor him in some other way. That approach, too, failed to bring results. So Dexter thought up a way to honor himself. He offered to pave the entire length of Newburyport's High Street at his own expense if only the town would rename the road Dexter Street. Town officials refused. Dexter then offered to build a new market building in downtown Newburyport if town officials would let him name it Dexter Hall. They would not.

Dexter seethed with anger at the rejections. He became even angrier when his wife agreed with the townspeople. She didn't think her nutty husband deserved to have anything named after him either. Dexter decided to get revenge on his wife in a most unusual way. He turned her into a ghost. He simply got up one morning in 1795 and declared her dead. From that day on, he referred to her as "Mrs. Dexter, the ghost that was my wife," or simply "the ghost." And although she continued to live with Dexter until his death in 1806, he never again acknowledged her presence.

As far as Newburyport was concerned, he showed them. He left town, taking his money and his "ghost" with him. He moved to Chester, New Hampshire, a town that he believed would appreciate his importance. The people of Newburyport breathed a sigh of relief as they watched him go. At last, it seemed, they were free of the bothersome Timothy Dexter. But a year later, Dexter returned. Apparently life in Chester hadn't turned out the way he

had hoped it would. The local minister had condemned his drinking habits, and the state had taxed him heavily. Still, one good thing had happened to Dexter in New Hampshire. He had become a lord.

No one knows quite how he came by the title, but when he returned to Newburyport, he claimed to be "the first lord in America, the first Lord Dexter." He bought a stately mansion near the center of town. Then he settled down to live in the manner of an English nobleman. He imported expensive furniture, rugs, and artwork from Europe. He hired a poet to write poems praising him. He even commissioned a sculptor to create forty painted wooden statues for his lawn. The statues were life-size likenesses of some of the world's greatest figures. They included George Washington, Benjamin Franklin, the emperor of China, and, of course, Timothy Dexter himself. Dexter ordered an inscription to be carved at the base of his statue. It read, "I am the first in the East, the first in the West, and the greatest philosopher in the Western World."

Soon tourists clogged the street in front of Dexter's home to view the brightly colored statues. Even that, however, did not satisfy "Lord" Dexter. He wanted to take one last stab at fame. He decided to write a book explaining his personal philosophy and telling the story of his life.

In just a few weeks in 1802, he composed his masterpiece. He called it *A Pickle for the Knowing Ones*.

The people of Newburyport, who by then thought they had seen it all, were amazed. Dexter had not used a single punctuation mark in his book. The whole thing was one long sentence, without commas, semicolons, or periods. At the end of the book, however, Dexter provided two solid pages of punctuation marks. He instructed his readers to sprinkle them "like salt and pepper" wherever they wanted in the text. Dexter's book did not become a best-seller, but it did make people pay attention to Timothy Dexter, one more time. And he did achieve fame of a sort, even if it is not quite the kind of fame he had in mind. ■

If you have been timed while reading this selection, enter your reading time below. Then turn to the Words per Minute table on page 155 and look up your reading speed (words per minute). Enter your reading speed on the graph on page 156.

READING TIME: Unit 11
_____ : _____
Minutes   *Seconds*

How well did you read?

- *Answer the four types of questions that follow. The directions for each type of question tell you how to mark your answers.*

- *When you have finished all four exercises, check your work by using the answer key on page 151. For each right answer, put a check mark (✔) on the line beside the box. For each wrong answer, write the correct answer on the line.*

- *For scoring each exercise, follow the directions below the questions.*

A FINDING THE MAIN IDEA

Look at the three statements below. One expresses the main idea of the story you just read. A good main idea statement answers two questions: it tells *who* or *what* is the subject of the story, and it answers the understood question *does what?* or *is what?* Another statement is *too broad*, it is vague and doesn't tell much about the topic of the story. The third statement is *too narrow*, it tells about only one part of the story.

Match the statements with the three answer choices below by writing the letter of each answer in the box in front of the statement it goes with.

M—Main Idea   B—Too Broad   N—Too Narrow

_____ ☐ 1. Timothy Dexter made himself a fortune from some odd business schemes, but angered and annoyed his neighbors by his strange behavior.

_____ ☐ 2. Timothy Dexter drew a lot of attention because of his unusual behavior.

_____ ☐ 3. Timothy Dexter made a fortune by shipping warming pans and mittens to the West Indies.

_____ Score 15 points for a correct *M* answer
_____ Score 5 points for each correct *B* or *N* answer

_____ TOTAL SCORE: Finding the Main Idea

B RECALLING FACTS

How well do you remember the facts in the story you just read?
Put an x in the box in front of the correct answer to each of the
multiple choice questions below.

1. In the West Indies, Dexter's warming pans were
   bought
   ___ ☐ a. by Russian merchants.
   ___ ☐ b. for use as molasses skimmers.
   ___ ☐ c. by a man from Newcastle, England.

2. Dexter began his strange schemes and behavior
   around
   ___ ☐ a. 1970.
   ___ ☐ b. 1870.
   ___ ☐ c. 1790.

3. When Dexter returned to Newburyport after living in
   Chester, New Hampshire, he claimed to be
   ___ ☐ a. emperor of the United States.
   ___ ☐ b. the first lord in America.
   ___ ☐ c. governor of New Hampshire.

4. Dexter hired a sculptor to carve
   ___ ☐ a. an enormous marble statue of Mrs. Dexter.
   ___ ☐ b. a statue of himself for the Newburyport town green.
   ___ ☐ c. forty wooden statues for his lawn.

5. Timothy Dexter's book, *A Pickle for the Knowing
   Ones,* contained no
   ___ ☐ a. punctuation.
   ___ ☐ b. words.
   ___ ☐ c. capital letters.

Score 5 points for each correct answer

___ TOTAL SCORE: Recalling Facts

C MAKING INFERENCES

An inference is a judgment that is made or an idea that is
arrived at based on facts or on information that is given. You
make an inference when you understand something that is *not*
stated directly, but that is *implied,* or suggested by the facts that
are given.

Below are five statements that are judgments or ideas that
have been arrived at from the facts of the story. Write the letter
C in the box in front of each statement that is a correct inference. Write the letter F in front of each faulty inference.

C—Correct Inference   F—Faulty Inference

___ ☐ 1. Timothy Dexter believed himself to be a wise
        man.

___ ☐ 2. Dexter had few friends in Newburyport.

___ ☐ 3. Mrs. Dexter didn't respect her husband.

___ ☐ 4. The people of Newburyport admired the statues
        Dexter put on his lawn.

___ ☐ 5. *A Pickle for the Knowing Ones* has come to be
        considered an important philosophical work.

Score 5 points for each correct answer

___ TOTAL SCORE: Making Inferences

D USING WORDS PRECISELY

Each of the numbered sentences below contains an underlined word or phrase from the story you have just read. Under the sentence are three definitions. One has the *same* meaning as the underlined word or phrase, one has *almost the same* meaning, and one has the *opposite* meaning. Match the definitions with the three answer choices by writing the letter that stands for each answer in the box in front of the definition it goes with.

S—Same   A—Almost the Same   O—Opposite

1. The people of Newburyport sat underlined smugly back and waited.

___ ☐ a. in a self-satisfied way

___ ☐ b. encouragingly

___ ☐ c. conceitedly

2. He bought a stately mansion near the center of town.

___ ☐ a. small and simple

___ ☐ b. grand

___ ☐ c. showy

3. He felt that his newfound wealth entitled him to the respect and admiration of his peers.

___ ☐ a. gave a right

___ ☐ b. disqualified

___ ☐ c. legalized

4. Dexter seethed with anger at the rejection.

___ ☐ a. stayed calm

___ ☐ b. fumed

___ ☐ c. exploded

5. He even commissioned a sculptor to create forty painted wooden statues for his lawn.

___ ☐ a. dismissed

___ ☐ b. hired

___ ☐ c. appointed

___ Score 3 points for each correct *S* answer

___ Score 1 point for each correct *A* or *O* answer

___ TOTAL SCORE: Using Words Precisely

● *Enter the four total scores in the spaces below, and add them together to find your Critical Reading Score. Then record your Critical Reading Score on the graph on page 157.*

___	Finding the Main Idea
___	Recalling Facts
___	Making Inferences
___	Using Words Precisely
___	CRITICAL READING SCORE: Unit 11

Bill Veeck seriously believed that baseball should be fun to watch. When his teams played, the fans never knew what to expect. Veeck's antics did sometimes prompt frowns (or worse) from others involved in the sport, but the peanut-buyers in the bleachers were always entertained.

Bill Veeck: Entertaining the Fans

"For the Browns, number one-eighth, Eddie Gaedel, batting for Saucier." The public address announcer said it, but no one could believe it. The umpire certainly didn't believe it. He took one look at Gaedel and stormed over to the Browns' dugout, demanding to know what was going on. When he found out, he tried his best not to laugh. Gaedel had a perfectly legal major league baseball contract. The three-foot seven-inch midget really planned to pinch-hit for center fielder Frank Saucier of the St. Louis Browns.

Bobby Cain, pitcher for the Detroit Tigers, looked at Gaedel in disbelief. The St. Louis fans roared with delight. How could Cain throw strikes to a midget? Well, he couldn't. He threw Gaedel four straight high pitches, walking him. Another player immediately went out to first base to run in Gaedel's place. Gaedel simply jogged off the field to the cheers of the fans, never again to appear in a major league baseball game. Bill Veeck (pronounced VEK), the owner of the St. Louis Browns, had pulled off another shameless stunt.

Baseball writers across the country let Veeck know what they thought of his latest gimmick. Some called it "shameful," "cheap," and a "mockery of the sport." Joe Williams, a writer for the *New York World-Telegram*, wrote, "What Veeck calls showmanship can more often be accurately identified as vulgarity." The next day, August 20, 1951, the American League barred midgets from major league baseball. Will Harridge, president of the American League, then tried to wipe Eddie Gaedel's name from the record book. But Veeck, who had promised baseball immortality to his small friend, raised a storm of protest. He reminded Harridge that Gaedel had a legal contract, and that the game was official. Besides, if Gaedel hadn't played, then who had batted for Saucier? Harridge quickly realized that removing the midget's name from the record would be more trouble than it was worth. Gaedel's name remains in the record book to this day.

Bill Veeck always said that "the fan is king." He believed baseball belonged to the fans and should be fun. His way of making the game fun was to do flamboyant things to entertain the folks in the stands.

Veeck bought his first team, the minor league Milwaukee Brewers, in 1941. The Brewers were "absolutely the worst team I had ever seen," said Veeck. Their record was nineteen wins and forty-three losses when he took control. When Veeck went to his first game as owner, he found exactly twenty-two fans in the stands. Clearly, something had to be done to draw more people into the ballpark.

Veeck decided to woo the public with colorful promotions. He used whatever tricks, gifts, and bargains he could think of to lure people to see the Brewers. He even organized his own jazz band to

Eddie Gaedel is the only midget ever to play in a major league baseball game. Veeck arranged for his day on the diamond. Some people were not amused.

entertain the fans. The band members included the team's manager, its radio announcer, its business manager, and Veeck himself. A fifth member of the band was an awful pitcher who just happened to be an excellent violin player. Veeck kept him with the team to play the violin, not to pitch. Whenever the game got a little dull, the band would wander through the stands serenading the fans.

Veeck also loved to give away weird door prizes. He just wanted to see how the lucky winner would react. Once he presented six live baby pigeons to the most dignified man he could find in the ballpark. Veeck wanted to see how the man would hold on to six birds while watching a ball game. The poor man gave it a good try. He lost three pigeons in the early innings, but did manage to keep the other three by holding one in each hand and the third between his knees. For being such a good sport, Veeck later sent the man a dozen fully-dressed game birds, ready for the oven.

On one occasion, Veeck awarded a fan the worst swaybacked horse he could find. Another fan won a dozen live lobsters, still in their cages. The lobsters spent the entire nine innings trying to crawl out of the cages. The unfortunate fan spent the time shoving them back in.

Veeck owned the Brewers during World War II. Wartime production kept factories open around the clock. Many women worked the night shift, seven days a week. One day a couple of female factory workers complained to Veeck that they never got to see any games because they were all played at night. So Veeck scheduled a special "Rosie the Riveter" morning game starting at 9:00 A.M. Any woman who arrived at the park wearing a hard hat or a welding mask got free admission. The ushers dressed in nightgowns and nightcaps and served free coffee and doughnuts.

Veeck also had some outlandish schemes for the game itself. He once installed a chicken wire screen above the rightfield fence. That turned the opposition's home runs into singles or doubles, as the balls bounced off the screen. Whenever the Brewers came to bat, Veeck rolled the screen out of the way. The league outlawed that practice after just one game.

In 1943 Veeck joined the Marines. He lost a leg during the war and had to be fitted with a wooden leg. But such a handicap could hardly slow down a man like Veeck. After the war, he got back into baseball. During his baseball career, he owned four different major league teams.

He never stopped dreaming up fantastic stunts to entice new fans to the ballpark. One day he gave away twenty thousand orchids. Another day he presented ten thousand cupcakes to a woman just to see how much space they would occupy in her kitchen. Once, when he owned the St. Louis Browns, he even let the fans call the plays. Whenever the manager was supposed to make a major decision, Veeck held up signs suggesting possible choices. Whichever choice drew the most cheers from the crowd was what the manager would do. The Browns actually won the game.

During his forty-five-year career in baseball, Veeck managed to offend just about everyone in the game at one time or another. But he did draw people to the ballparks. And he did leave his mark on the sport. Although a couple of his teams regularly finished at the bottom, two were real winners and had tremendous fan support. In 1948 his Cleveland Indians drew over 2.6 million fans, breaking the major league attendance record. The Indians won the American League pennant and the World Series that year. On that team was Larry Doby, the first black player in the American League, whom Veeck had hired. In 1959, Veeck's Chicago White Sox won the pennant and set a club attendance record, drawing over 1.6 million fans. The great sportswriter Red Smith once wrote, "Veeck was born into baseball and belongs there." ■

If you have been timed while reading this selection, enter your reading time below. Then turn to the Words per Minute table on page 155 and look up your reading speed (words per minute). Enter your reading speed on the graph on page 156.

READING TIME: Unit 12

_____ : _____
Minutes   *Seconds*

How well did you read?

- *Answer the four types of questions that follow. The directions for each type of question tell you how to mark your answers.*

- *When you have finished all four exercises, check your work by using the answer key on page 151. For each right answer, put a check mark (✔) on the line beside the box. For each wrong answer, write the correct answer on the line.*

- *For scoring each exercise, follow the directions below the questions.*

answer key on page 151

A FINDING THE MAIN IDEA

Look at the three statements below. One expresses the main idea of the story you just read. A good main idea statement answers two questions: it tells *who* or *what* is the subject of the story, and it answers the understood question *does what?* or *is what?* Another statement is *too broad,* it is vague and doesn't tell much about the topic of the story. The third statement is *too narrow,* it tells about only one part of the story.

Match the statements with the three answer choices below by writing the letter of each answer in the box in front of the statement it goes with.

M—Main Idea   **B—Too Broad**   **N—Too Narrow**

____ ☐ 1. Bill Veeck, the owner of several major league baseball teams, was an outrageous character.

____ ☐ 2. Bill Veeck used outrageous stunts to create publicity for his baseball teams and to entertain the fans.

____ ☐ 3. Bill Veeck often got himself in trouble with baseball officials.

____ Score 15 points for a correct *M* answer
____ Score 5 points for each correct *B* or *N* answer

____ TOTAL SCORE: Finding the Main Idea

B RECALLING FACTS

How well do you remember the facts in the story you just read?
Put an *x* in the box in front of the correct answer to each of the
multiple choice questions below.

1. Eddie Gaedel was
   - ___ ☐ a. a midget.
   - ___ ☐ b. an umpire.
   - ___ ☐ c. the owner of the Milwaukee Brewers.

2. To entertain the fans, Veeck organized his own
   - ___ ☐ a. bridge tournament.
   - ___ ☐ b. jazz band.
   - ___ ☐ c. boxing matches.

3. While he was in the United States Marine Corps, Veeck
   - ___ ☐ a. bought the Chicago White Sox.
   - ___ ☐ b. wrote articles for the *New York World-Telegram.*
   - ___ ☐ c. lost a leg.

4. Once Veeck gave a woman ten thousand cupcakes just to see
   - ___ ☐ a. how many of them she could eat.
   - ___ ☐ b. how much space they would take up in her kitchen.
   - ___ ☐ c. how she would hang on to them all during the game.

5. Veeck's career in baseball lasted
   - ___ ☐ a. ten years.
   - ___ ☐ b. twenty-five years.
   - ___ ☐ c. forty-five years.

Score 5 points for each correct answer

___ TOTAL SCORE: Recalling Facts

C MAKING INFERENCES

An inference is a judgment that is made or an idea that is
arrived at based on facts or on information that is given. You
make an inference when you understand something that is *not*
stated directly, but that is *implied,* or suggested by the facts that
are given.

Below are five statements that are judgments or ideas that
have been arrived at from the facts of the story. Write the letter
C in the box in front of each statement that is a correct inference. Write the letter *F* in front of each faulty inference.

C—Correct Inference   F—Faulty Inference

___ ☐ 1. Most team owners took the game of baseball more seriously than Bill Veeck did.

___ ☐ 2. Today midgets are allowed to play on American League baseball teams.

___ ☐ 3. Eddie Gaedel knew that he would only get to play in one game.

___ ☐ 4. "Rosie the Riveter" was the nickname given to women who worked in factories during World War II.

___ ☐ 5. Bill Veeck enjoyed losing teams more than winning teams.

Score 5 points for each correct answer

___ TOTAL SCORE: Making Inferences

D USING WORDS PRECISELY

Each of the numbered sentences below contains an underlined word or phrase from the story you have just read. Under the sentence are three definitions. One has the *same* meaning as the underlined word or phrase, one has *almost the same* meaning, and one has the *opposite* meaning. Match the definitions with the three answer choices by writing the letter that stands for each answer in the box in front of the definition it goes with.

S—Same   **A—Almost the Same**   **O—Opposite**

1. Bill Veeck, the owner of the St. Louis Browns, had pulled off another <u>shameless</u> stunt.

____ ☐ a. respectable

____ ☐ b. bold and immodest

____ ☐ c. disgraceful

2. His way of making the game fun was to do <u>flamboyant</u> things to entertain the folks in the stands.

____ ☐ a. flashy

____ ☐ b. unusual

____ ☐ c. conservative

3. Veeck decided to <u>woo</u> the public with colorful promotions.

____ ☐ a. try to attract

____ ☐ b. persuade

____ ☐ c. discourage

4. Veeck also had some <u>outlandish</u> schemes for the game itself.

____ ☐ a. commonplace

____ ☐ b. outrageous

____ ☐ c. original

5. He never stopped dreaming up fantastic stunts to <u>entice</u> new fans to the ballpark.

____ ☐ a. tempt

____ ☐ b. lure

____ ☐ c. repel

____ Score 3 points for each correct *S* answer

____ Score 1 point for each correct *A* or *O* answer

____ TOTAL SCORE: Using Words Precisely

● *Enter the four total scores in the spaces below, and add them together to find your Critical Reading Score. Then record your Critical Reading Score on the graph on page 157.*

_____ Finding the Main Idea

_____ Recalling Facts

_____ Making Inferences

_____ Using Words Precisely

_____ CRITICAL READING SCORE: Unit 12

Ludwig II of Bavaria was less in touch
with the needs of his kingdom and
subjects than he was with the fantasies
that unfolded within his own head. He
saw the world not as it was, but as
he wanted it to be. Ludwig loved music,
theater, and beautiful things. His fantasies
inspired him to build one of the most
fantastic castles in the world. They also
led to a conspiracy to dethrone him.
Ludwig's end was both sad and
mysterious.

The Dream King

No one ever said that King Ludwig II of Bavaria lacked a lively imagination. Once, in 1865, he had his bedroom ceiling painted with an orchard of orange trees against a blue sky. Then he commanded his servants to install an artificial moon and a rainbow. The king liked to fantasize that he was sleeping in a beautiful garden.

Ludwig's days were filled with fanciful illusions. So were many of his nights. Often, around 8:00 P.M., Ludwig would order a groom to bring him his horse. Pretending it was early morning, he would set off on a ride. But he never went far. For six or seven hours, the king would ride around and around the small track at the riding school. Every so often he would change horses. Ludwig imagined that he was actually going to some particular German town. In fact, he calculated the exact distance according to the circumference of the track. After a few hours in the saddle, the king would stop, and his servants would bring him a picnic supper. When Ludwig had finished his meal, he would remount his horse and continue riding in circles until he'd figured he had reached his "destination." After a hard day's ride, the king would retire to his bedroom around 3:00 A.M.

Obviously, Ludwig had an active fantasy life. Largely for that reason, Ludwig II, who ruled Bavaria from 1864 to 1886, became known as the "Dream King."

When Ludwig went to his country residence, he continued his night rides. On those occasions, however, he was not constrained by a riding track. The king's wild midnight excursions became legend in the Bavarian Alps. On even the coldest winter nights, the peasants would hear sleigh bells ringing as Ludwig's golden sleigh rushed beneath their windows. The coachmen and outriders wore bright, gaudy uniforms, while Ludwig huddled in his huge fur coat.

Extremely shy, Ludwig did not enjoy the company of other people. In the last years of his reign, he almost always dined alone. Still, the royal servants regularly set the table for three or four people. Ludwig would imagine that he was dining with kings who lived long ago. At times he talked to those dead monarchs as if they were actually his guests.

If Ludwig didn't like people, he did have a certain fondness for horses. He once invited his favorite mare to dine with him. Ludwig's servants prepared a sumptuous meal of soup, fish, a roast, and wine. After the horse had eaten her share, she proceeded to smash the valuable china and crystal. Ludwig just looked on and smiled.

Ludwig loved the theater. But the audiences made him uncomfortable by gawking at him instead of watching the plays. So he finally insisted on private performances. The only plays that really interested him dealt with life in the French court during the seventeenth and eighteenth centuries. So he commanded the actors to perform old plays, long out of date. Ludwig even went so far as to hire local playwrights to write new plays about the French court.

Such eccentricities were harmless. What really got Ludwig into trouble and led to his downfall was his mania for building castles. Every king is entitled to a castle or two. But Ludwig built three in his life of only forty years. As a child Ludwig created dream castles with toy blocks. As king he could afford to build real ones. Most kings build castles as monuments to themselves. Ludwig, however, built them as a hobby. He simply loved castles. He would dream of a certain kind of castle and then decide to build it.

His most famous castle, Neuschwanstein, is an elaborate fairy-tale castle perched on a mountain pinnacle. It is nearly inaccessible. A special road had to be built to reach the site. Water had to be hauled up from the valley below. In addition, twenty feet of rocky summit had to be blasted away to make enough level space for the castle. The excessive cost of Neuschwanstein and his other two castles never bothered Ludwig. Even when war broke out in 1870, work on the castle continued uninterrupted. Ludwig could withdraw from the affairs of state and live in his own private world at Neuschwanstein.

But the splendor of his castles could not shield the king forever. Bavaria simply couldn't afford Ludwig's boundless castle building. And the country couldn't afford to have a king who totally neglected his official duties. At last certain high officials conspired to remove Ludwig from the throne. In January 1886, they began to hatch their plot. Ludwig's uncle and heir, Prince Luitpold von Bayern, ordered doctors to declare Ludwig incurably insane and unable to rule. On January 12, the prince ordered that Ludwig be confined at Schloss Berg, a castle just outside the capital of Munich. Ludwig might have been able to fight back by rousing people in his support, for he was well loved by many of his subjects. But he continued to live in his fantasy world. He took no steps to save himself.

The very next day, Ludwig and his physician went for an afternoon walk down by the lake. When several hours passed and the men did not return, a couple of policemen began a search. When darkness fell, a full-scale search of the area began. About 10:00 P.M. someone spotted a black object floating in the lake. It was the king's overcoat. A half hour later, the searchers fished out the bodies of the two men. The Dream King was dead. Was it an accident? Murder? Suicide? No one knows for sure. How and why Ludwig II died remains one of the unsolved mysteries of history. ■

If you have been timed while reading this selection, enter your reading time below. Then turn to the Words per Minute table on page 155 and look up your reading speed (words per minute). Enter your reading speed on the graph on page 156.

READING TIME: Unit 13

——— : ———
Minutes   *Seconds*

How well did you read?

- *Answer the four types of questions that follow. The directions for each type of question tell you how to mark your answers.*

- *When you have finished all four exercises, check your work by using the answer key on page 151. For each right answer, put a check mark (✔) on the line beside the box. For each wrong answer, write the correct answer on the line.*

- *For scoring each exercise, follow the directions below the questions.*

A FINDING THE MAIN IDEA

Look at the three statements below. One expresses the main idea of the story you just read. A good main idea statement answers two questions: it tells *who* or *what* is the subject of the story, and it answers the understood question *does what?* or *is what?* Another statement is *too broad*, it is vague and doesn't tell much about the topic of the story. The third statement is *too narrow*, it tells about only one part of the story.

Match the statements with the three answer choices below by writing the letter of each answer in the box in front of the statement it goes with.

M—Main Idea   **B—Too Broad**   **N—Too Narrow**

___ ☐ 1. Ludwig II was a Bavarian king who had unusual ways.

___ ☐ 2. King Ludwig II did outlandish things that interfered with his governing of Bavaria.

___ ☐ 3. King Ludwig II often took long horseback rides to nowhere.

___ Score 15 points for a correct *M* answer

___ Score 5 points for each correct *B* or *N* answer

___ TOTAL SCORE: Finding the Main Idea

B RECALLING FACTS

How well do you remember the facts in the story you just read? Put an *x* in the box in front of the correct answer to each of the multiple choice questions below.

1. Ludwig was known as
   - ____ ☐ a. the Castle King.
   - ____ ☐ b. the Horse King.
   - ____ ☐ c. the Dream King.

2. Ludwig was very
   - ____ ☐ a. short.
   - ____ ☐ b. shy.
   - ____ ☐ c. practical.

3. Ludwig liked to pretend he was eating with
   - ____ ☐ a. monarchs who had died long ago.
   - ____ ☐ b. peasants from the Bavarian Alps.
   - ____ ☐ c. French actors.

4. Neuschwanstein was one of Ludwig's
   - ____ ☐ a. best friends.
   - ____ ☐ b. favorite mares.
   - ____ ☐ c. castles.

5. In 1886, Ludwig's uncle ordered doctors to declare Ludwig
   - ____ ☐ a. an impostor.
   - ____ ☐ b. insane.
   - ____ ☐ c. king.

Score 5 points for each correct answer

____ TOTAL SCORE: Recalling Facts

C MAKING INFERENCES

An inference is a judgment that is made or an idea that is arrived at based on facts or on information that is given. You make an inference when you understand something that is *not* stated directly, but that is *implied*, or suggested by the facts that are given.

Below are five statements that are judgments or ideas that have been arrived at from the facts of the story. Write the letter *C* in the box in front of each statement that is a correct inference. Write the letter *F* in front of each faulty inference.

C—Correct Inference   F—Faulty Inference

- ____ ☐ 1. Ludwig was a poor ruler.

- ____ ☐ 2. Ludwig had many children.

- ____ ☐ 3. Ludwig's castles have fallen to ruin since the Dream King's death.

- ____ ☐ 4. Ludwig never ate meat.

- ____ ☐ 5. Ludwig was the best-loved king in Bavarian history.

Score 5 points for each correct answer

____ TOTAL SCORE: Making Inferences

D USING WORDS PRECISELY

Each of the numbered sentences below contains an underlined word or phrase from the story you have just read. Under the sentence are three definitions. One has the *same* meaning as the underlined word or phrase, one has *almost the same* meaning, and one has the *opposite* meaning. Match the definitions with the three answer choices by writing the letter that stands for each answer in the box in front of the definition it goes with.

S—Same   A—Almost the Same   O—Opposite

1. Ludwig's days were filled with <u>fanciful</u> illusions.

   ____ ☐ a. creative

   ____ ☐ b. realistic

   ____ ☐ c. imaginative

2. On those occasions, however, he was not <u>constrained</u> by a riding track.

   ____ ☐ a. held back

   ____ ☐ b. encouraged

   ____ ☐ c. interfered with

3. Ludwig's servants prepared a <u>sumptuous</u> meal of soup, fish, a roast, and wine.

   ____ ☐ a. magnificent

   ____ ☐ b. expensive

   ____ ☐ c. plain

4. His most famous castle is Neuschwanstein—an elaborate fairy-tale castle perched on a mountain <u>pinnacle</u>.

   ____ ☐ a. peak

   ____ ☐ b. valley

   ____ ☐ c. ridge

5. It is nearly <u>inaccessible</u>. A special road had to be built to reach the site.

   ____ ☐ a. approachable

   ____ ☐ b. unavailable

   ____ ☐ c. unreachable

____ Score 3 points for each correct *S* answer

____ Score 1 point for each correct *A* or *O* answer

____ TOTAL SCORE: Using Words Precisely

• *Enter the four total scores in the spaces below, and add them together to find your Critical Reading Score. Then record your Critical Reading Score on the graph on page 157.*

_____	Finding the Main Idea
_____	Recalling Facts
_____	Making Inferences
_____	Using Words Precisely
_____	CRITICAL READING SCORE: Unit 13

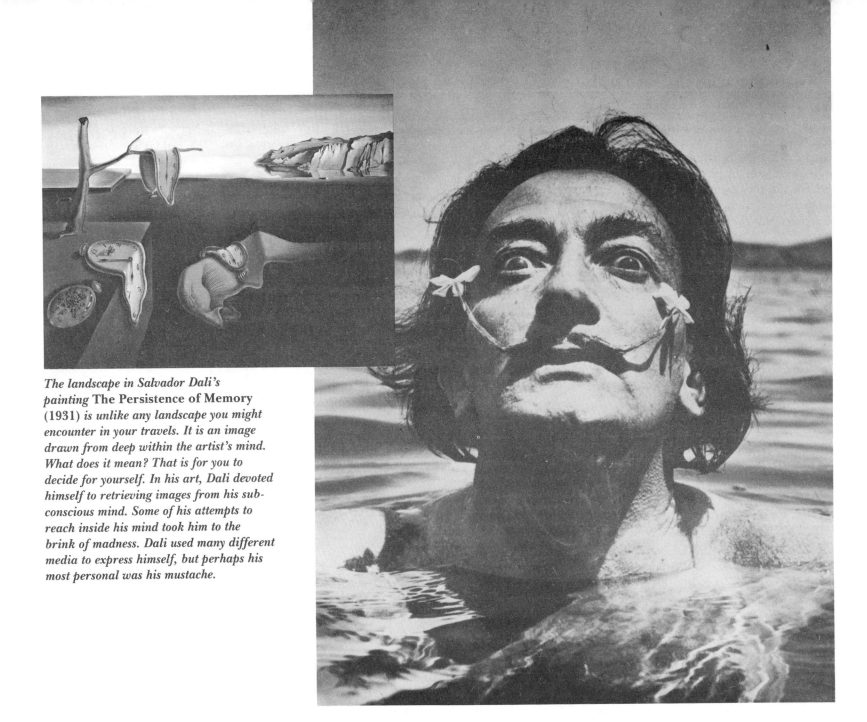

The landscape in Salvador Dali's
painting **The Persistence of Memory**
(1931) *is unlike any landscape you might
encounter in your travels. It is an image
drawn from deep within the artist's mind.
What does it mean? That is for you to
decide for yourself. In his art, Dali devoted
himself to retrieving images from his subconscious mind. Some of his attempts to
reach inside his mind took him to the
brink of madness. Dali used many different
media to express himself, but perhaps his
most personal was his mustache.*

Salvador Dali: A Question of Reality

Strange things happen in Salvador Dali's paintings. Fried eggs hang from strings. Trees grow out of pianos. Human bodies melt into violins. Horses burst from cannon barrels. Giant grasshoppers pop up everywhere, clinging to birds, boxes, human faces. What does it all mean? It is a glimpse into the artist's mind. It is Dali's contribution to surrealism. Surrealism is art that explores subconscious thoughts and images. The surrealists believed that the subconscious—the inner mind—held the greatest reality. Surreal means reality above reality. The surrealists created strange, dreamlike pictures to express the contents of their own subconscious minds. Dali was one of the masters of surrealism.

Salvador Dali's career as an artist spanned more than sixty years. Born in Spain in 1904, he began painting when he was just a young boy. In 1918 he held his first public exhibition. He went on to national and then international fame. He produced hundreds of masterpieces. At times he worked incredibly slowly. He once spent six months painting a still life of a loaf of bread. On other occasions, though, fantastic, dreamlike images simply welled up inside him. When that happened, Dali could work very quickly. He stated that he did not consciously create those images. He simply recorded them as they came to him. In fact, he once admitted that even he did not understand the meanings of many of them.

Dali was not only a painter. He pursued other creative avenues with equal flair. In the 1930s he produced stunning costumes for a ballet company. He designed eerie landscapes for the movie set of Alfred Hitchcock's famous film *Spellbound*. He wrote complex poems and essays. He designed jewelry, furniture, and clothing. He even ventured into filmmaking. His first film was a French silent movie produced in 1929. It was called *Un Chien Andalou*. Although it lasted only seventeen minutes, its shocking surrealist approach made it unforgettable. It featured such powerful but violent images as a razor splitting open an eye.

It did not take long for Dali to earn a reputation in the art world. Everyone could see that he was a man driven by a strange inner force. It was that force that led him to produce his wild but compelling works. He never used drugs. He believed that drugs would only interfere with his attempts to capture subconscious visions. He did, however, go to great lengths to summon those visions. He believed that they would rise up within him if he was properly prepared to receive them. Once he locked himself in a small, damp room for two solid months. He kept the shutters closed the entire time, and lit the room with only one electric light bulb. He wanted to create an environment that would remind him of his mother's womb. He hoped to trigger subconscious memories of his life before birth. He would then translate the images of those memories onto canvas.

Dali's artistic eccentricities also exhibited themselves beyond his studio walls. He often engaged in public antics. Many resulted in front-page headlines. Perhaps he was trying to get publicity for himself and his work. Perhaps he was simply reacting to his own unique perspective on the world. In any case, some of his actions became legendary.

Once, for instance, he greeted reporters in a strange way. He met them waving an eight-foot-long stick of bread. Another time he appeared in public wearing a tuxedo, which at first glance was unexceptional. A closer look, however, showed that he had pinned artificial flies all over the tux. For an exhibit opening in Paris, he once arrived in a Rolls-Royce. That in itself was not unusual. What was unusual was that the car was filled with cauliflower.

In 1936 Dali's creative antics nearly led

to disaster. At the beginning of a lecture in London, he startled his audience by walking onstage in a full underwater diving suit. As he began speaking, everyone listened with great eagerness. They all hoped to gain insights into the master's work. After a few minutes, though, the audience began to look perplexed. No one could understand what Dali was saying. As he went on, his speech became more and more garbled. Soon he began making frantic gestures with his hands. Still the audience sat, unsure what it all meant. Finally some people realized what was happening. Trapped inside the airtight diver's suit, Dali could not breathe. He was suffocating before their eyes. Quickly they rushed to free him. They managed to pull off the diver's helmet just before he fainted.

Despite that harrowing experience, Dali continued his outrageous behavior. In 1939 he went to New York to design a window display for a Fifth Avenue department store. The display included a fur-lined bathtub filled with water. He finished his work on the window late at night. The next morning he returned to the store to admire his creation. In the meantime, though, someone had gone in and made changes in the display. Dali was so infuriated that he climbed up into the display area and tipped over the bathtub, causing it to crash through the window. As water and glass flew all around him, he jumped down onto the pavement and stormed away.

In the 1940s, Dali began doing unusual things with his mustache. He let it grow very long, then used wax to mold it into odd shapes. Sometimes he twisted it into a figure eight. Sometimes he fashioned it to look like the horns of a bull. Sometimes he even dipped one end into paint and used it as a paintbrush.

Dali never lost his love for absurdity. By the 1980s, though, he had no strength left for zaniness. In 1982 his beloved wife Gala died. In 1984 a fire in his bedroom left him with such serious burns that he required skin grafts. After that, he went to live in seclusion in his home town of Figueras, Spain. From his quarters there, he could oversee the Teatro-Museo Dali, a museum devoted to his works.

The museum houses many classic Dali images. It includes paintings of elephants on stilts and portraits of people with holes cut in their chests. In one room sits an old Cadillac. It is part of a display called *Rainy Taxi*. If someone drops a coin into a slot, rain will begin falling inside the car. No guidebook is available to help viewers make sense of the art in the museum. Dali felt that each viewer had to reach his or her own conclusions about the meanings of the works.

For most people, it is difficult to comprehend all the messages contained within Dali's works. It is even more confusing when we take into account Dali's bizarre personal behavior. How should we assess him? Was he a genius who acted crazy? Or was he a crazy man who possessed genius? Perhaps Dali himself offered the best clue back in 1934. He said, "The only difference between myself and a madman is that I am not mad." ■

If you have been timed while reading this selection, enter your reading time below. Then turn to the Words per Minute table on page 155 and look up your reading speed (words per minute). Enter your reading speed on the graph on page 156.

READING TIME: Unit 14	
_____ : _____	
Minutes	*Seconds*

How well did you read?

- *Answer the four types of questions that follow. The directions for each type of question tell you how to mark your answers.*

- *When you have finished all four exercises, check your work by using the answer key on page 151. For each right answer, put a check mark (✔) on the line beside the box. For each wrong answer, write the correct answer on the line.*

- *For scoring each exercise, follow the directions below the questions.*

A FINDING THE MAIN IDEA

Look at the three statements below. One expresses the main idea of the story you just read. A good main idea statement answers two questions: it tells *who* or *what* is the subject of the story, and it answers the understood question *does what?* or *is what?* Another statement is *too broad*, it is vague and doesn't tell much about the topic of the story. The third statement is *too narrow*, it tells about only one part of the story.

Match the statements with the three answer choices below by writing the letter of each answer in the box in front of the statement it goes with.

M—Main Idea   B—Too Broad   N—Too Narrow

____ ☐ 1. Salvador Dali's life was an extension of the bizarre, dreamlike art he created.

____ ☐ 2. Salvador Dali was an unusually imaginative twentieth-century artist.

____ ☐ 3. Salvador Dali was one of the masters of surrealistic painting.

____ Score 15 points for a correct *M* answer

____ Score 5 points for each correct *B* or *N* answer

____ TOTAL SCORE: Finding the Main Idea

B RECALLING FACTS

How well do you remember the facts in the story you just read? Put an *x* in the box in front of the correct answer to each of the multiple choice questions below.

1. Dali spent six months working on a painting of
   - ___ ☐ a. an elephant on stilts.
   - ___ ☐ b. trees growing out of pianos.
   - ___ ☐ c. a loaf of bread.

2. Dali never
   - ___ ☐ a. used drugs.
   - ___ ☐ b. wore a tuxedo.
   - ___ ☐ c. created violent images.

3. Dali almost suffocated in
   - ___ ☐ a. an underwater diving suit.
   - ___ ☐ b. a car filled with cauliflower.
   - ___ ☐ c. the small, damp room where he worked.

4. Dali's 1939 department store display included
   - ___ ☐ a. ballet costumes he had designed.
   - ___ ☐ b. an old Cadillac.
   - ___ ☐ c. a fur-lined bathtub.

5. Dali sometimes made a figure eight out of
   - ___ ☐ a. paintbrushes.
   - ___ ☐ b. jewelry.
   - ___ ☐ c. his mustache.

Score 5 points for each correct answer

___ TOTAL SCORE: Recalling Facts

C MAKING INFERENCES

An inference is a judgment that is made or an idea that is arrived at based on facts or on information that is given. You make an inference when you understand something that is *not* stated directly, but that is *implied,* or suggested by the facts that are given.

Below are five statements that are judgments or ideas that have been arrived at from the facts of the story. Write the letter *C* in the box in front of each statement that is a correct inference. Write the letter *F* in front of each faulty inference.

C—Correct Inference   F—Faulty Inference

- ___ ☐ 1. Dali preferred jewelry-making to filmmaking.
- ___ ☐ 2. Dali had few friends.
- ___ ☐ 3. Dali enjoyed startling people.
- ___ ☐ 4. Dali was better known as a filmmaker and set designer than as a painter.
- ___ ☐ 5. Dali liked to attract attention to himself.

Score 5 points for each correct answer

___ TOTAL SCORE: Making Inferences

D USING WORDS PRECISELY

Each of the numbered sentences below contains an underlined word or phrase from the story you have just read. Under the sentence are three definitions. One has the *same* meaning as the underlined word or phrase, one has *almost the same* meaning, and one has the *opposite* meaning. Match the definitions with the three answer choices by writing the letter that stands for each answer in the box in front of the definition it goes with.

S—Same   A—Almost the Same   O—Opposite

1. On other occasions, though, fantastic, dreamlike images simply <u>welled</u> up inside him.

    ____ ☐ a. rose

    ____ ☐ b. dwindled

    ____ ☐ c. appeared

2. Everyone could see that he was a man <u>driven</u> by a strange inner force.

    ____ ☐ a. pushed along

    ____ ☐ b. guided

    ____ ☐ c. held back

3. It was that force that led him to produce his wild but <u>compelling</u> works.

    ____ ☐ a. weak

    ____ ☐ b. forceful

    ____ ☐ c. interesting

4. Perhaps he was simply reacting to his own unique <u>perspective</u> on the world.

    ____ ☐ a. point of view

    ____ ☐ b. ignorance

    ____ ☐ c. opinion

5. By the 1980s, though, he had no strength left for <u>zaniness</u>.

    ____ ☐ a. seriousness

    ____ ☐ b. humor

    ____ ☐ c. kooky behavior

____ Score 3 points for each correct *S* answer
____ Score 1 point for each correct *A* or *O* answer
____ TOTAL SCORE: Using Words Precisely

● *Enter the four total scores in the spaces below, and add them together to find your Critical Reading Score. Then record your Critical Reading Score on the graph on page 157.*

_____ Finding the Main Idea
_____ Recalling Facts
_____ Making Inferences
_____ Using Words Precisely
_____ **CRITICAL READING SCORE: Unit 14**

GROUP THREE

Norton I, Emperor of the United States

Joshua Abraham Norton didn't have a royal bone in his body. He also had no college education, no permanent home, and no money. He wasn't even a citizen of the United States. None of that seemed to bother the forty-year-old Englishman, however, when in 1859 he boldly declared himself emperor of the United States.

When Norton moved to the United States in 1849, he had no plans to become emperor. He left England because he had heard about the California gold rush. Gold had been discovered in California, and people were swarming into San Francisco in hopes of striking it rich. Norton figured that he could make money selling scarce goods to the miners. For a while that's just what he did. He set up a shop in downtown San Francisco, in which he sold coffee, tea, flour, and rice. By 1853 he had accumulated a fortune. Then disaster struck. Norton lost all his savings in one bad investment. On top of that, a fire tore through his warehouses, destroying his entire supply of goods. Almost overnight, Joshua Norton found himself bankrupt.

The sudden loss of his fortune shattered Norton, making him feel like a total failure. For a while he worked as a clerk for a Chinese rice company. But such low-level work felt humiliating to him after

the freedom and power of being on top. So he quit his job, gave up his fancy living quarters, and moved into a cheap little boardinghouse. There he stayed, day after day, alone with his thoughts.

Friends who visited him found him tense and depressed at first. The depression faded after a while, but in its place appeared something quite bizarre. Norton began to talk more and more about the political problems of the United States. He saw that the bitter arguments over slavery were leading the country toward civil war. His solution to the problem caught his friends off guard. What the United States needed, Norton began to say, was an emperor. Only an emperor could prevent war and restore peace and harmony to the country. As Norton rambled on, it became clear whom he had in mind for the job.

On September 17, 1859, Norton went public with his idea. He walked into the newsroom of the *San Francisco Bulletin* and handed the editor a written notice, asking that it be published in the next edition of the newspaper. At the "request and desire of a large majority of the citizens of these United States," the announcement stated, "I, Joshua Norton, . . . declare and proclaim myself emperor of these United States. . . ." It was signed "NORTON I,

Emperor of the United States."

The editor of the *Bulletin* must have found the notice amusing, for he ran it on the front page. There it captured people's attention, and soon everyone in town was talking about the new "emperor." A few days later, Norton made his first public appearance. He dressed in an old blue military uniform, complete with brass buttons and red trim. At his side he wore a heavy sword that he had had custom-made at a blacksmith shop. Then he proudly set out through the streets of San Francisco, greeting everyone he met with a solemn nod.

Perhaps people recognized that Norton was basically harmless, or perhaps they sensed how important it was to him to be taken seriously. Maybe they just liked the idea of having their own resident emperor. In any event, they responded to the appearance of Norton I with cheers. The warm welcome convinced Norton that his subjects deserved the very best government they could get. He decided that the members of Congress were too corrupt, so to the amazement of the people of San Francisco, he published a statement dissolving the Congress of the United States. He also announced that he was dissolving the Republic of the United States. No one in Washington, D.C., paid any attention

to Norton, but he didn't care. As long as the people in his own city treated him with respect, he was happy.

Norton did soon find, however, that running an empire could be quite expensive. After all, an emperor needs shoes, clothes, food, transportation, and lodging. He tried to solve his financial problems by printing his own money. He designed "bonds of the empire," which he declared to be worth fifty cents each. Many shopkeepers found the bonds amusing and agreed to let Norton use them. Still, the bonds did not cover all the royal expenses.

To augment his personal funds, Norton devised a system of taxation. He asked each business in the city to pay its fair share of taxes to the empire. He asked small businesses for twenty-five cents, and larger ones for two or three dollars. Everyone knew that the "taxes" Norton collected went straight into his own pocket, but when he appeared at their doors, all decked out in his royal uniform, few business owners had the heart to turn him down. On a good day Norton took in as much as twenty-five dollars in taxes.

Sometimes Norton asked for more than the usual amount of money. That happened whenever he came up with a grand new vision for promoting world peace. Such visions came to him regularly, and

Emperor Norton I reigned in San Francisco in the second half of the nineteenth century. Though little known outside that area, he was well loved and respected by his subjects there.

when they did, he would set out in search of financial backing. He would approach a loyal subject of the empire and ask for a loan of hundreds of millions of dollars. Although he never got the loan, he seemed just as happy to get a donation of a dime or two.

As emperor of the United States, Norton expected certain privileges. He expected, for example, to eat all his meals for free. He would simply appear at a restaurant, announce his identity, and wait for the management to serve him. Before long, every restaurant owner in San Francisco recognized Norton I. Like everyone else in the city, the restaurant owners found him charming. They always treated him courteously, offered him their best food, and never insulted him by asking him to pay.

Norton expected the empire to support him, and in a sense, it did. From 1859 until his death in 1880, a group of old friends paid his rent. Streetcar conductors paid his fares on trolley cars, and his landlord paid his laundry bills. The Central Pacific Railroad issued him a lifetime pass to all its California dining and sleeping cars. And the San Francisco Board of Supervisors voted unanimously to foot the bill for a new set of royal clothes.

Despite the way it may sound, Emperor Norton I did not live a carefree life. Many serious problems weighed heavily on his mind. He worried, for example, about the fate of Mexico. He finally decided that Mexico was "entirely unfit to manage her own affairs," so he appointed himself "Protector of Mexico." When the Civil War broke out, Norton felt it was his responsibility to end it. He ordered Abraham Lincoln and Jefferson Davis, the leader of the South, to go to California so he could make peace between them. He could never understand why the two men ignored his command.

Norton had many other, smaller, duties as well. He felt obligated to wander the city inspecting the streets and water drains. He checked his watch constantly to be sure the streetcars in his empire were running on schedule. He felt he had to attend a different church every Sunday to prevent jealousy among the congregations. And he attended every public meeting to offer his imperial words of wisdom.

Sometimes he used the public meetings to seek help on the issues that troubled him most. During one meeting, for instance, he rose and asked the crowd the following question: "Take twenty-five square miles of land. Let it rain on that land twenty-four hours. Then turn every one of those drops of water into a baby. How many babies would there be?" He became furious when the bewildered audience could not provide an answer.

Finally he just stormed out of the meeting.

Incidents such as that one proved to Norton I that his poor lovable subjects simply weren't very bright. That insight made him even more determined to take good care of them.

Apparently, the people of San Francisco felt that Norton was a good emperor. When he died after having ruled his empire for twenty-one years, the entire city went into mourning. His subjects spent ten thousand dollars on his funeral. Eight thousand people filed past his casket. Newspapers wrote loving tributes to him. One newspaper summed up his appeal this way: "The Emperor Norton killed nobody, robbed nobody and deprived nobody of his country—which is more than can be said for most fellows in his trade." ■

If you have been timed while reading this selection, enter your reading time below. Then turn to the Words per Minute table on page 155 and look up your reading speed (words per minute). Enter your reading speed on the graph on page 156.

READING TIME: Unit 15

_____ : _____
Minutes   *Seconds*

How well did you read?

- *Answer the four types of questions that follow. The directions for each type of question tell you how to mark your answers.*

- *When you have finished all four exercises, check your work by using the answer key on page 152. For each right answer, put a check mark (✓) on the line beside the box. For each wrong answer, write the correct answer on the line.*

- *For scoring each exercise, follow the directions below the questions.*

A FINDING THE MAIN IDEA

Look at the three statements below. One expresses the main idea of the story you just read. A good main idea statement answers two questions: it tells *who* or *what* is the subject of the story, and it answers the understood question *does what?* or *is what?* Another statement is *too broad,* it is vague and doesn't tell much about the topic of the story. The third statement is *too narrow,* it tells about only one part of the story.

Match the statements with the three answer choices below by writing the letter of each answer in the box in front of the statement it goes with.

M—Main Idea   **B—Too Broad**   **N—Too Narrow**

_____ ☐ 1. For twenty-one years, Joshua Norton lived as though he was emperor of the United States.

_____ ☐ 2. Joshua Norton worried a great deal about the political problems of the country.

_____ ☐ 3. Joshua Norton was under the delusion that he was a top figure in the government of the United States.

_____ Score 15 points for a correct *M* answer

_____ Score 5 points for each correct *B* or *N* answer

_____ TOTAL SCORE: Finding the Main Idea

B RECALLING FACTS

How well do you remember the facts in the story you just read? Put an *x* in the box in front of the correct answer to each of the multiple choice questions below.

1. Norton originally emigrated to the United States to
____ ☐ a. make money during the gold rush.
____ ☐ b. declare himself emperor.
____ ☐ c. create a new system of taxation.

2. After losing all his money in 1853, Norton became a
____ ☐ a. bartender in a saloon.
____ ☐ b. clerk for a Chinese rice company.
____ ☐ c. streetcar conductor.

3. Norton proclaimed himself emperor
____ ☐ a. while visiting Washington, D.C.
____ ☐ b. in the *San Francisco Bulletin*.
____ ☐ c. in a letter to the leader of Mexico.

4. Norton planned to end the Civil War by
____ ☐ a. inviting Abraham Lincoln and Jefferson Davis to hold peace talks with him.
____ ☐ b. leading Mexico in an invasion of the United States.
____ ☐ c. having all the country's leaders meet in San Francisco for a peace rally.

5. Emperor Norton
____ ☐ a. never went to church.
____ ☐ b. always went to the same church.
____ ☐ c. went to a different church every Sunday.

Score 5 points for each correct answer

____ TOTAL SCORE: Recalling Facts

C MAKING INFERENCES

An inference is a judgment that is made or an idea that is arrived at based on facts or on information that is given. You make an inference when you understand something that is *not* stated directly, but that is *implied*, or suggested by the facts that are given.

Below are five statements that are judgments or ideas that have been arrived at from the facts of the story. Write the letter *C* in the box in front of each statement that is a correct inference. Write the letter *F* in front of each faulty inference.

C—Correct Inference   F—Faulty Inference

____ ☐ 1. Most of the people who went to San Francisco during the gold rush were from England.

____ ☐ 2. Norton never came up with a realistic plan for ensuring world peace.

____ ☐ 3. People in Mexico paid no attention to Norton's declaration that he was "Protector of Mexico."

____ ☐ 4. Joshua Norton never married.

____ ☐ 5. Small children were afraid of Emperor Norton.

Score 5 points for each correct answer

____ TOTAL SCORE: Making Inferences

D USING WORDS PRECISELY

Each of the numbered sentences below contains an underlined word or phrase from the story you have just read. Under the sentence are three definitions. One has the *same* meaning as the underlined word or phrase, one has *almost the same* meaning, and one has the *opposite* meaning. Match the definitions with the three answer choices by writing the letter that stands for each answer in the box in front of the definition it goes with.

S—Same   A—Almost the Same   O—Opposite

1. He decided that the members of Congress were too <u>corrupt</u>, so to the amazement of the people of San Francisco, he dissolved the Congress.

____ ☐ a. pure

____ ☐ b. evil

____ ☐ c. dishonest

2. To <u>augment</u> his personal funds, Norton devised a system of taxation.

____ ☐ a. add to

____ ☐ b. cut back

____ ☐ c. extend

3. Such visions came to him regularly, and when they did, he would set out in search of financial <u>backing</u>.

____ ☐ a. advice

____ ☐ b. attacks

____ ☐ c. support

4. Sometimes he used the public meetings to seek help on the <u>issues</u> that troubled him most.

____ ☐ a. topics

____ ☐ b. problems

____ ☐ c. accepted ideas

5. That <u>insight</u> made him even more determined to take good care of them.

____ ☐ a. idea

____ ☐ b. realization

____ ☐ c. oversight

____ Score 3 points for each correct S answer
____ Score 1 point for each correct A or O answer

____ TOTAL SCORE: Using Words Precisely

- *Enter the four total scores in the spaces below, and add them together to find your Critical Reading Score. Then record your Critical Reading Score on the graph on page 157.*

_____ Finding the Main Idea
_____ Recalling Facts
_____ Making Inferences
_____ Using Words Precisely

_____ CRITICAL READING SCORE: Unit 15

Charles Johnson thinks that the world is filled with gullible fools—people who will believe anything that is fed to them by politicians and the news media. The most outrageous lie the world has been fed, he believes, is that the earth is round. Charles and his wife, Marjory, moved to a remote desert area in California to avoid having to deal with round earthers. From their outpost they run the Flat Earth Society and devise experiments to prove the earth is flat.

Charles Johnson and the Flat Earth Society

The earth does not revolve around the sun, the space shuttle cannot orbit the earth, and no man has ever set foot on the moon. Those are some of the proclamations made by a California man named Charles K. Johnson. Johnson is absolutely serious when he makes such remarks. And he speaks not as just a private citizen, but as president of the Flat Earth Society.

Like the rest of us, Charles Johnson grew up in a society that held that the earth was round. Johnson, however, refused to accept that idea. He declared that common sense tells us that the earth has to be flat. "Australians do *not*," he said, "hang by their feet under the world . . . ." As Johnson grew older, his adamant belief in a flat earth led him to certain other conclusions. He determined, for example, that the earth does not move at all. It does not "whirl, spin, or gyrate." He reckoned, however, that the sun and the moon *do* move around, traveling in circular patterns high above the earth's plane. To Johnson, sunrise and sunset are nothing more than optical illusions. He figures that the sun and moon are each about thirty-two miles in diameter, and he judges them to be roughly three thousand miles away from the earth, or the distance from Boston to San Francisco.

As for the earth, Johnson claims that no one can be sure of its exact outline. The way he sees it, the North Pole is at the center of the great plane that is the earth, and surrounding it are the inhabited regions of the world. Beyond the known landscape looms a great wall of ice, which Johnson estimates to be 150 feet high. Since no one has ever gotten past it, no one knows what, if anything, lies beyond.

Charles Johnson is not the first person to subscribe to such offbeat theories. He stands out, however, because he has managed to turn his unorthodox beliefs into a career. The Flat Earth Society has been around since 1956, but when Johnson took over as president in 1971, it had only a few members. Under Johnson's care, the society has grown to include several hundred members. Johnson receives two thousand letters of inquiry each year, and the society is still growing. Annual dues are ten dollars, and Johnson makes each new member sign a statement pledging not to "harm, degrade, damage or defame" the society.

With the help of his wife, Marjory, Charles Johnson puts out a quarterly newsletter called *Flat Earth News*. In it, he condemns the "weird, way-out occult concoction of gibberish" known as modern science. According to Johnson, science is "unrelated to the real world of facts, technology and inventions, tall buildings and fast cars, airplanes and other Real and Good things in life. . . ."

Johnson also uses his newsletter to report on the experiments that he and Marjory conduct from time to time. On one occasion, for example, they reasoned that if the earth were really round, then all large bodies of water would have to be convex—curved like the outer surface of a ball. So they checked out Lake Tahoe, in Nevada. They took the fact that they could not detect any bulging or curving of the water's surface as further proof of the validity of their flat earth theory.

Johnson knows that many people consider him crazy, but he expects that. He believes that only a small group of elite people have the intelligence to see the true nature of the world. The rest of humanity is nothing but a herd of unthinking, uncaring animals. And, he states, the Flat Earth Society does not want members who are "stupid, mindless brute beasts with two feet." Johnson even has his own version of history to back up his views. According to him, Christopher Columbus believed that the earth was flat. His crew, on the other hand, worried about sailing down over the curve of a round earth.

Johnson also asserts that George Washington believed the earth was flat.

Washington, he says, joined in the American Revolution in order to escape England's round earth doctrine. The way Johnson tells it, even Franklin Roosevelt knew the earth was flat. Johnson thinks that Roosevelt planned to usher in a whole new world order as soon as World War II ended. Roosevelt planned to use the United Nations to get himself elected president of the world and then officially declare the earth flat. The only reason the plan didn't work was that Roosevelt died before the war ended.

Johnson takes his theory one step further, claiming that today's top government officials all know the earth is not round. They are afraid, he says, to make that fact known for fear that such a revelation would free people's minds. That, in turn, might cause politicians to lose some of their power. So Johnson maintains that the governments of the world are all engaged in a great conspiracy, trying to cover up the fact that the earth is flat.

Johnson sees the 1969 *Apollo* landing on the moon in that light. Television footage of Neil Armstrong walking on the moon did not shake Johnson's beliefs in the least. He remains certain that the whole episode was faked by Hollywood producers in order to fool the American public. He scorns those who were taken in by such an obvious sham.

To protect his integrity, Johnson finds it necessary to isolate himself from the swarming masses of round earthers. He and his wife live on a remote piece of land near Lancaster, California. Their house sits on a hill half a mile from the nearest neighbor. The area is so far from a center of civilization that they have no electricity. They also do without running water. From that quiet and remote headquarters, Charles Johnson continues to make his voice heard. His ultimate goal is to force the government to end its charade and admit that the earth is not round. His efforts may fall flat, but he is determined to keep trying. ∎

If you have been timed while reading this selection, enter your reading time below. Then turn to the Words per Minute table on page 155 and look up your reading speed (words per minute). Enter your reading speed on the graph on page 156.

READING TIME: Unit 16

_____ : _____
Minutes   *Seconds*

How well did you read?

- *Answer the four types of questions that follow. The directions for each type of question tell you how to mark your answers.*

- *When you have finished all four exercises, check your work by using the answer key on page 152. For each right answer, put a check mark (✓) on the line beside the box. For each wrong answer, write the correct answer on the line.*

- *For scoring each exercise, follow the directions below the questions.*

A | FINDING THE MAIN IDEA

Look at the three statements below. One expresses the main idea of the story you just read. A good main idea statement answers two questions: it tells *who* or *what* is the subject of the story, and it answers the understood question *does what?* or *is what?* Another statement is *too broad,* it is vague and doesn't tell much about the topic of the story. The third statement is *too narrow,* it tells about only one part of the story.

Match the statements with the three answer choices below by writing the letter of each answer in the box in front of the statement it goes with.

M—Main Idea   B—Too Broad   N—Too Narrow

_____ ☐ 1. Charles Johnson, head of the Flat Earth Society, firmly believes the earth is flat.

_____ ☐ 2. Charles Johnson, who lives in Lancaster, California, does not trust modern scientists or government officials.

_____ ☐ 3. Charles Johnson publishes a newsletter called *Flat Earth News.*

_____ Score 15 points for a correct *M* answer

_____ Score 5 points for each correct *B* or *N* answer

_____ TOTAL SCORE: Finding the Main Idea

B RECALLING FACTS

How well do you remember the facts in the story you just read? Put an *x* in the box in front of the correct answer to each of the multiple choice questions below.

1. Charles Johnson believes that the moon
   - ____ ☐ a. moves.
   - ____ ☐ b. does not move.
   - ____ ☐ c. does not exist.

2. Each year, Charles Johnson receives two thousand
   - ____ ☐ a. death threats.
   - ____ ☐ b. letters asking about the Flat Earth Society.
   - ____ ☐ c. pictures of the *Apollo* moon landing.

3. Marjory and Charles Johnson live in a house with no
   - ____ ☐ a. roof.
   - ____ ☐ b. electricity.
   - ____ ☐ c. windows.

4. Johnson thinks the 1969 moon landing was staged by
   - ____ ☐ a. Hollywood producers.
   - ____ ☐ b. Franklin Roosevelt.
   - ____ ☐ c. British scientists.

5. Johnson believes that situated at the center of the earth's flat plane is
   - ____ ☐ a. Lake Tahoe.
   - ____ ☐ b. the South Pole.
   - ____ ☐ c. the North Pole.

Score 5 points for each correct answer

____ TOTAL SCORE: Recalling Facts

C MAKING INFERENCES

An inference is a judgment that is made or an idea that is arrived at based on facts or on information that is given. You make an inference when you understand something that is *not* stated directly, but that is *implied*, or suggested by the facts that are given.

Below are five statements that are judgments or ideas that have been arrived at from the facts of the story. Write the letter *C* in the box in front of each statement that is a correct inference. Write the letter *F* in front of each faulty inference.

C—Correct Inference   F—Faulty Inference

- ____ ☐ 1. Johnson believes he is smarter than most people.
- ____ ☐ 2. Johnson thinks that all politicians are dishonest.
- ____ ☐ 3. Johnson is accumulating acceptable scientific evidence to support his theories.
- ____ ☐ 4. Charles and Marjory Johnson believe only in what they can see and touch for themselves.
- ____ ☐ 5. Johnson does not believe that Australia is a real country.

Score 5 points for each correct answer

____ TOTAL SCORE: Making Inferences

D USING WORDS PRECISELY

Each of the numbered sentences below contains an underlined word or phrase from the story you have just read. Under the sentence are three definitions. One has the *same* meaning as the underlined word or phrase, one has *almost the same* meaning, and one has the *opposite* meaning. Match the definitions with the three answer choices by writing the letter that stands for each answer in the box in front of the definition it goes with.

S—Same   A—Almost the Same   O—Opposite

1. As Johnson grew older, his <u>adamant</u> belief in a flat earth led him to certain other conclusions.

___ ☐ a. flexible

___ ☐ b. unyielding

___ ☐ c. sure

2. He <u>determined</u>, for example, that the earth does not move at all.

___ ☐ a. considered

___ ☐ b. doubted

___ ☐ c. concluded

3. Charles Johnson is not the first person to <u>subscribe</u> to such offbeat theories.

___ ☐ a. believe

___ ☐ b. disagree with

___ ☐ c. listen to

4. They took the fact that they could not detect any bulging or curving of the water's surface as further proof of the <u>validity</u> of their flat earth theory.

___ ☐ a. acceptability

___ ☐ b. truth

___ ☐ c. falsity

5. His ultimate goal is to force the government to end its <u>charade</u> and admit that the earth is not round.

___ ☐ a. story

___ ☐ b. game of pretense

___ ☐ c. truthfulness

___ Score 3 points for each correct *S* answer
___ Score 1 point for each correct *A* or *O* answer

___ TOTAL SCORE: Using Words Precisely

● *Enter the four total scores in the spaces below, and add them together to find your Critical Reading Score. Then record your Critical Reading Score on the graph on page 157.*

_____	Finding the Main Idea
_____	Recalling Facts
_____	Making Inferences
_____	Using Words Precisely
_____	**CRITICAL READING SCORE: Unit 16**

Swinging an ax and shouting passages from the Bible, Carry Nation enforced the Kansas prohibition law by forcibly— and single-handedly—closing down a good number of the saloons in Kansas. Her campaign was, literally, a smashing success.

Carry Nation: Fighting the "Hellish Poison"

Mr. Dobson didn't know what hit him. On June 6, 1900, Carry Amelia Nation stormed into his saloon in Kiowa, Kansas. In a clear, calm voice, Carry told the customers, "I have come to save you from a drunkard's fate." She then proceeded to destroy the place.

Although she was fifty-four years old at the time, Carry was still a ruggedly built woman. Nearly six feet tall, she weighed 175 pounds and had extremely muscular arms. As the patrons watched in stunned silence, Carry set her imposing strength loose on poor Mr. Dobson's saloon. Heaving brick after brick, she smashed every mirror, glass, and bottle in the place. Then she slapped her hands together and looked the shocked proprietor straight in the eye. "Now, Mr. Dobson," she said, "I have finished. God be with you."

Carry had nothing personal against Mr. Dobson. She just hated liquor and the establishments that served that "hellish poison." Carry's first husband, Dr. Charles Gloyd, had been addicted to whiskey and had drunk himself to death in 1869, after only two years of marriage. That set Carry on the road to becoming an outspoken advocate of prohibition.

In 1877, Carry married David Nation, a journalist, lawyer, and minister. Her religious beliefs grew stricter and stronger,

and she took her new name, Carry A. Nation, as a sign that she was destined to help improve the moral welfare of the country. In 1890, she began to speak against the evils of liquor and to pray outside saloons. She soon combined her prayers with action.

On June 5, 1900, Carry had a dream in which a voice commanded her: "Take something in your hands and throw it at those places and smash them!" That was all Carry needed to hear. The next morning she picked up several dozen bricks, hitched up her horse to her buggy, and drove straight to Mr. Dobson's saloon.

After trashing that bar, she got back into her buggy and started to drive away, when suddenly a wonderful idea popped into her head. She still had a lot of bricks left, so with a gleam in her eye, she hurled two of them through Mr. Dobson's front windows. Then she went on to demolish two more saloons in Kiowa before finally running out of ammunition. Because she wanted to draw public attention to her campaign, she made no effort to leave town, and even demanded that the sheriff arrest her. The bewildered sheriff refused to do that. Carry had caught the town so off-guard that no one knew quite what to make of her or what to do with her.

You see, under Kansas law, liquor and

the saloons that served it were illegal. The police, however, generally ignored the law, and saloons flourished in every city and town in the state. Carry Nation had written letters of protest to the governor and to all the local newspapers, but nothing had come of her efforts. Finally, since the saloons were illegal, Carry decided that she was perfectly within her rights in destroying them.

Flushed with success, Carry extended her rampage to include every saloon in Kansas. She headed off to Wichita, the liquor capital of the state, where wholesale liquor warehouses and saloons abounded. Since she considered saloon-smashing a serious and honorable business, she dressed for the occasion. She wore a black dress with pearl buttons, square-toed shoes, and a black bonnet with a silk ribbon tied under her chin.

After surveying all the saloons in Wichita, Carry decided to start by taking on the most elegant one of all. It was situated in the basement of the Hotel Carey. Carry walked into the saloon and threw a brick through the huge mirror that hung over the bar. Then, with relentless determination, she destroyed the pictures of partially-clothed women that decorated the walls. Finally, she took out a foot-long iron bar and smashed all the bottles and glasses behind the bar. Just as the last bottle hit the floor, the police arrived.

"Madam," declared one officer, "I must arrest you for defacing property. "Defacing?" she cried. "Defacing? I am defacing nothing! I am *destroying*."

After a short stay in the local jail, Carry was released. By that time she had become the most notorious woman in the United States. Many people condemned her as a nut, but there were a considerable number who shared her hatred of alcohol. Every day Carry received hundreds of letters and telegrams congratulating her on her noble work. That, of course, only encouraged her to seek out new saloons to wreck. After her jail stint, she began using a distinctive new weapon: a hatchet. Carry used it not only to break mirrors and bottles, but also to hack at the wooden bars—the counters—themselves.

Carry Nation raided dozens of saloons in Kansas and neighboring states. Sometimes she was accompanied by women who sang hymns as she smashed. Other times she worked alone, singing, praying, and shouting passages from the Bible at the patrons of the bar. Smart saloon owners either closed their doors when Carry was in the neighborhood or hired armed guards to keep her outside. Still, she made many successful raids.

The police arrested her over thirty times, usually on the grounds of "disturbing the peace." Often the judge would fine her for damages or ask her to leave town. To raise money to pay her numerous fines, Carry gave speeches and sold souvenir autographed hatchets. She railed not only against liquor but also against tobacco, corsets, and "improper" dress for women (short skirts), all of which she considered evils of society. Her work inspired other "hatchet women" to attack the bars in their neighborhoods.

Gradually, though, the excitement Carry stirred up began to die down. People grew tired of her unique brand of lawlessness. Many peaceful members of anti-liquor groups wanted nothing to do with her. Carry tried to rekindle the fires of moral outrage by giving lectures in the United States and Europe. But more often than not the audience would greet her with hoots and showers of rotten vegetables rather than with applause.

Still, Carry continued to strike saloons from time to time. In 1909 she attacked a barroom in Washington's Union Depot with three hatchets she called Faith, Hope, and Charity. In January 1910, in Butte, Montana, she hit her last saloon. In that bar Carry Nation met her match: a powerful young woman named May Maloy. When Carry tried to force her way into May's saloon, May gave her a sound beating. After that, Carry retired her hatchets, and the saloonkeepers of the Midwest breathed a long sigh of relief. ∎

If you have been timed while reading this selection, enter your reading time below. Then turn to the Words per Minute table on page 155 and look up your reading speed (words per minute). Enter your reading speed on the graph on page 156.

┌─────────────────────────────────────┐
│ READING TIME: Unit 17   │
│ ─────────── : ───────────   │
│ *Minutes*   *Seconds*   │
└─────────────────────────────────────┘

How well did you read?

- *Answer the four types of questions that follow. The directions for each type of question tell you how to mark your answers.*

- *When you have finished all four exercises, check your work by using the answer key on page 152. For each right answer, put a check mark (✔) on the line beside the box. For each wrong answer, write the correct answer on the line.*

- *For scoring each exercise, follow the directions below the questions.*

check your work by using the answer key on page 152.

A · FINDING THE MAIN IDEA

Look at the three statements below. One expresses the main idea of the story you just read. A good main idea statement answers two questions: it tells *who* or *what* is the subject of the story, and it answers the understood question *does what?* or *is what?* Another statement is *too broad,* it is vague and doesn't tell much about the topic of the story. The third statement is *too narrow,* it tells about only one part of the story.

Match the statements with the three answer choices below by writing the letter of each answer in the box in front of the statement it goes with.

M—Main Idea   B—Too Broad   N—Too Narrow

____ ☐ 1. Carry Nation fought the sale of liquor by wrecking saloons.

____ ☐ 2. Carry Nation used violence in her campaign against drinking.

____ ☐ 3. Carry Nation often used a hatchet to smash saloons.

____ Score 15 points for a correct *M* answer

____ Score 5 points for each correct *B* or *N* answer

____ TOTAL SCORE: Finding the Main Idea

B RECALLING FACTS

How well do you remember the facts in the story you just read? Put an x in the box in front of the correct answer to each of the multiple choice questions below.

1. Carry did most of her saloon-smashing in
   - ☐ a. Kansas.
   - ☐ b. Washington.
   - ☐ c. New York.

2. Carry's first husband was
   - ☐ a. the sheriff of Wichita.
   - ☐ b. addicted to whiskey.
   - ☐ c. killed by a bartender.

3. Carry came up with an idea of saloon-smashing after hearing
   - ☐ a. a speech by the editor of her local newspaper.
   - ☐ b. her husband preach against alcohol.
   - ☐ c. a voice in a dream.

4. The police
   - ☐ a. never arrested Carry.
   - ☐ b. arrested Carry over thirty times.
   - ☐ c. often beat Carry.

5. Faith, Hope, and Charity were the names Carry gave to three
   - ☐ a. saloons she destroyed.
   - ☐ b. hatchets.
   - ☐ c. governors who supported her efforts.

Score 5 points for each correct answer

____ TOTAL SCORE: Recalling Facts

C MAKING INFERENCES

An inference is a judgment that is made or an idea that is arrived at based on facts or on information that is given. You make an inference when you understand something that is *not* stated directly, but that is *implied,* or suggested by the facts that are given.

Below are five statements that are judgments or ideas that have been arrived at from the facts of the story. Write the letter C in the box in front of each statement that is a correct inference. Write the letter F in front of each faulty inference.

C—Correct Inference   F—Faulty Inference

____ ☐ 1. Her second husband, David Nation, supported Carry in her anti-liquor campaign.

____ ☐ 2. When Carry Nation was on her rampage, Kansas was the only state in the country that had laws prohibiting the sale of alcohol.

____ ☐ 3. The Hotel Carey was an elegant place.

____ ☐ 4. Carry did not want anyone to know that it was she who was smashing saloons.

____ ☐ 5. Most saloonkeepers were afraid of Carry Nation.

Score 5 points for each correct answer

____ TOTAL SCORE: Making Inferences

D USING WORDS PRECISELY

Each of the numbered sentences below contains an underlined word or phrase from the story you have just read. Under the sentence are three definitions. One has the *same* meaning as the underlined word or phrase, one has *almost the same* meaning, and one has the *opposite* meaning. Match the definitions with the three answer choices by writing the letter that stands for each answer in the box in front of the definition it goes with.

S—Same   A—Almost the Same   O—Opposite

1. As the patrons watched in stunned silence, Carry set her <u>imposing</u> strength loose on poor Mr. Dobson's saloon.

   ____ ☐ a. ordinary

   ____ ☐ b. impressive

   ____ ☐ c. majestic

2. That set Carry on the road to becoming an outspoken <u>advocate</u> of prohibition.

   ____ ☐ a. enemy

   ____ ☐ b. promoter

   ____ ☐ c. defender

3. She headed off to Wichita, the liquor capital of the state, where wholesale liquor warehouses and saloons <u>abounded</u>.

   ____ ☐ a. were plentiful

   ____ ☐ b. were scarce

   ____ ☐ c. existed

4. By that time she had become the most <u>notorious</u> woman in the United States.

   ____ ☐ a. unfavorably famous

   ____ ☐ b. familiar

   ____ ☐ c. little known

5. Carry tried to <u>rekindle</u> the fires of moral outrage by giving lectures in the United States and Europe.

   ____ ☐ a. put an end to

   ____ ☐ b. keep in motion

   ____ ☐ c. stir up again

____ Score 3 points for each correct *S* answer

____ Score 1 point for each correct *A* or *O* answer

____ TOTAL SCORE: Using Words Precisely

● *Enter the four total scores in the spaces below, and add them together to find your Critical Reading Score. Then record your Critical Reading Score on the graph on page 157.*

_____	Finding the Main Idea
_____	Recalling Facts
_____	Making Inferences
_____	Using Words Precisely
_____	CRITICAL READING SCORE: Unit 17

He jumped onto an alligator, kept strange pets in his bedroom, stuck his head between large, gaping jaws fringed with sharp teeth, and once bathed with owls. Charles Waterton found all animals intriguing. Eventually, it seems, he became a bit of a beast himself.

Charles Waterton Loved Animals

Charles Waterton loved animals—especially those creatures that other people found hideous. His favorites included vultures, buzzards, bats, and reptiles. Waterton kept numerous unconventional pets in his luxurious house in Yorkshire, England. He once sheltered a sloth in his bedroom for months because he felt sorry for the hairy little thing and figured it needed the company. He nurtured a whole collection of toads, and often spoke to them at great length, as though he were holding a conversation with them. And his day was not complete until he had kissed his chimpanzee.

Waterton could easily have spent his life scrutinizing animals in the laboratory of his thirty-acre estate. He had enough money to buy and care for a multitude of creatures, but Waterton didn't just want the animals brought to him—he wanted to go to them. He wanted to study them in their native surroundings. So in 1812, at the age of thirty, he shook off his comfortable life and set out for the jungles of Brazil.

Waterton had a wonderful time. He had such fun, in fact, that he returned to Brazil several times. On his most famous journey, in 1820, Waterton tramped through the tropical forests for months. He walked barefooted, for he believed shoes should be worn only indoors. Every now and then he would stop to cut stones, insects, and even infected chunks of flesh out of the soles of his feet. At night he strung a hammock between trees and grabbed a few hours' sleep.

One day he decided he wanted to examine an alligator. His native guide urged him to simply watch it from afar, but Waterton wanted to get a good, close look. He jumped recklessly onto the alligator's back and seized its front legs, holding tight while the beast thrashed about. Riding bareback on an alligator did not give Waterton a chance to conduct a detailed examination of the creature, but it did give him a mighty good sense of its incredible strength.

On another occasion, Waterton wanted to check out the teeth of a massive fourteen-foot jungle snake. Though the snake was not poisonous, it wasn't exactly harmless. It killed its victims by wrapping itself around them and crushing them to death. Waterton wasn't worried. When he spied the snake, he jumped on its tail and sat down. As the snake began to wrap him in its fatal hug, Waterton unhooked his suspenders and swiftly tied the snake up with them.

While in Brazil, Waterton learned of an amazing creature called the vampire bat.

According to local legend, the vampire bat lived exclusively on a diet of blood. When Waterton heard that, he became intrigued. He was determined to have a vampire bat bite him on his big toe, so he could see the bat in action.

Night after night, Waterton dangled his feet from his hammock, hoping a vampire bat would alight and feast on his toe. But though his guide was bitten repeatedly, Waterton was left with all toes intact. Could it be that the vampire bats found his scarred and filthy feet somewhat unappetizing?

Waterton finally gave up on the vampire bats and went home to England. All in all, his trip had been a great success. He had collected much valuable information and had become an expert on the creatures of the jungle. Eventually he even wrote a book, called *Wandering in South America*, detailing the events of his expedition.

Waterton married Anne Edmonstone in 1829, and it looked for a while as though he might settle down—perhaps even give up his obsession with animals. But a year later, after giving birth to a son, Anne died. Her death nearly broke Waterton's heart. Anne's two sisters moved in with Waterton, taking over care of the baby. Waterton felt lost and lonely. He could no longer bear to sleep in his bed because it

125

reminded him too much of Anne, so he took to sleeping on the floor, with a block of wood for a pillow. He also returned to his studies of animals.

Waterton became increasingly absorbed with the creatures, sometimes even seeming to forget that they were not human. Once, for example, on his way home from Italy, where he had gone to get some owls for his laboratory, he got the urge to take a bath. He decided that the owls might like to accompany him, reasoning that if a bath would invigorate him, it would certainly perk up the owls' spirits, too. So Waterton stopped at a bathhouse and carried the caged owls into the water with him. As it turned out, the owls did not share his enthusiasm for bathing. By the time Waterton was clean, many of the owls were drowned.

In all his years as a naturalist, Waterton found only one creature that he did not like: the black rat. A Roman Catholic, Waterton believed that the black rat was a Protestant weapon. He insisted that the rat had been smuggled into Catholic countries by German Protestants back in the Middle Ages to spread disease.

As the years passed, Waterton grew more and more eccentric. He once locked himself in a cage with a ferocious orangutan and stuck his head in the beast's mouth to examine its teeth. He gave it a hug, a kiss, and several pats on the head before finally leaving the cage. On another occasion, he became interested in how birds fly. After studying the wing structure of many birds, he built himself a giant set of wings, attached them to his shoulders, and climbed onto the roof of a building, fully intending to jump off and begin flapping his arms. Luckily, a group of friends spotted him and talked him out of his experiment.

Even age didn't slow Waterton down. At eighty, he astonished everyone by shinnying up a tree to inspect a hawk's nest in one of the topmost branches.

Of all Waterton's bizarre habits, however, one stood out as particularly strange.

Whenever a visitor arrived at his door, Waterton would sneak into the entrance hall and hide under a table. He would wait there until his guest headed for the coatrack. Then, without warning, he would growl like a savage dog, grab the visitor's leg with his teeth, and bite down viciously. It certainly was not the customary way of greeting people, but then Waterton wasn't your run-of-the-mill host. ■

If you have been timed while reading this selection, enter your reading time below. Then turn to the Words per Minute table on page 155 and look up your reading speed (words per minute). Enter your reading speed on the graph on page 156.

READING TIME: Unit 18
—————— : ——————
Minutes   *Seconds*

How well did you read?

- *Answer the four types of questions that follow. The directions for each type of question tell you how to mark your answers.*

- *When you have finished all four exercises, check your work by using the answer key on page 152. For each right answer, put a check mark (✔) on the line beside the box. For each wrong answer, write the correct answer on the line.*

- *For scoring each exercise, follow the directions below the questions.*

A FINDING THE MAIN IDEA

Look at the three statements below. One expresses the main idea of the story you just read. A good main idea statement answers two questions: it tells *who* or *what* is the subject of the story, and it answers the understood question *does what?* or *is what?* Another statement is *too broad*, it is vague and doesn't tell much about the topic of the story. The third statement is *too narrow*, it tells about only one part of the story.

Match the statements with the three answer choices below by writing the letter of each answer in the box in front of the statement it goes with.

M—Main Idea   **B—Too Broad**   **N—Too Narrow**

_____ ☐ 1. Charles Waterton kept many unusual animals on his large estate in England.

_____ ☐ 2. Charles Waterton did many strange and dangerous things involving animals.

_____ ☐ 3. Charles Waterton's greatest interest was animals.

_____ Score 15 points for a correct *M* answer

_____ Score 5 points for each correct *B* or *N* answer

_____ TOTAL SCORE: Finding the Main Idea

B RECALLING FACTS

How well do you remember the facts in the story you just read? Put an *x* in the box in front of the correct answer to each of the multiple choice questions below.

1. Waterton spent months tramping through the
   - ___ ☐ a. jungles of Brazil.
   - ___ ☐ b. Swiss Alps.
   - ___ ☐ c. Arabian desert.

2. Waterton slept with his feet dangling out of his hammock because he
   - ___ ☐ a. had a blood circulation problem.
   - ___ ☐ b. believed it would help keep away snakes.
   - ___ ☐ c. wanted a vampire bat to bite his toe.

3. Waterton accidentally killed some owls by
   - ___ ☐ a. putting them in cages.
   - ___ ☐ b. feeding them alligator meat.
   - ___ ☐ c. trying to give them a bath.

4. The one creature that Waterton did not like was the
   - ___ ☐ a. sloth.
   - ___ ☐ b. black vulture.
   - ___ ☐ c. black rat.

5. Waterton greeted his guests by
   - ___ ☐ a. handing them a jungle toad.
   - ___ ☐ b. growling and biting like a savage dog.
   - ___ ☐ c. locking them in a cage with an orangutan.

Score 5 points for each correct answer

___ TOTAL SCORE: Recalling Facts

C MAKING INFERENCES

An inference is a judgment that is made or an idea that is arrived at based on facts or on information that is given. You make an inference when you understand something that is *not* stated directly, but that is *implied*, or suggested by the facts that are given.

Below are five statements that are judgments or ideas that have been arrived at from the facts of the story. Write the letter *C* in the box in front of each statement that is a correct inference. Write the letter *F* in front of each faulty inference.

C—Correct Inference   F—Faulty Inference

- ___ ☐ 1. Charles Waterton spent his childhood in extreme poverty.
- ___ ☐ 2. Waterton had absolutely no fear of animals.
- ___ ☐ 3. Waterton spent no time with his son after his wife died.
- ___ ☐ 4. Charles Waterton was one of the most renowned and respected naturalists of the nineteenth century.
- ___ ☐ 5. Waterton was an intensely curious person.

Score 5 points for each correct answer

___ TOTAL SCORE: Making Inferences

D USING WORDS PRECISELY

Each of the numbered sentences below contains an underlined word or phrase from the story you have just read. Under the sentence are three definitions. One has the *same* meaning as the underlined word or phrase, one has *almost the same* meaning, and one has the *opposite* meaning. Match the definitions with the three answer choices by writing the letter that stands for each answer in the box in front of the definition it goes with.

S—Same   A—Almost the Same   O—Opposite

1. Waterton could easily have spent his life <u>scrutinizing</u> animals in the laboratory of his thirty-acre estate.

____ ☐ a. ignoring

____ ☐ b. studying carefully

____ ☐ c. watching

2. He jumped recklessly onto the alligator's back and seized its front legs, holding tight while the beast <u>thrashed</u> about.

____ ☐ a. tossed violently

____ ☐ b. struggled

____ ☐ c. held still

3. When Waterton heard that, he became <u>intrigued</u>.

____ ☐ a. bored

____ ☐ b. fascinated

____ ☐ c. interested

4. In 1829 Waterton married Anne Edmonstone, and it looked for a while as though he might settle down—perhaps even give up his <u>obsession</u> with animals.

____ ☐ a. lack of concern

____ ☐ b. curiosity

____ ☐ c. ruling passion

5. He decided that the owls might like to accompany him, reasoning that if a bath would <u>invigorate</u> him, it would certainly perk up the owls' spirits, too.

____ ☐ a. cheer up

____ ☐ b. refresh

____ ☐ c. weaken

____ Score 3 points for each correct *S* answer
____ Score 1 point for each correct *A* or *O* answer

____ **TOTAL SCORE:** Using Words Precisely

● *Enter the four total scores in the spaces below, and add them together to find your Critical Reading Score. Then record your Critical Reading Score on the graph on page 157.*

_____ Finding the Main Idea
_____ Recalling Facts
_____ Making Inferences
_____ Using Words Precisely

_____ **CRITICAL READING SCORE: Unit 18**

People trusted Ferdinand Demara, though they didn't know that was his name. He was amiable, intelligent, and good at what he did—whatever it was. He changed careers many times, was successful in all of them, and trained for none. How did he manage it? He was a great impostor.

The Great Impostor

Dr. Joseph Cyr took a deep breath, then reached down into his patient's open chest wound and pulled out a bullet. He worked slowly and carefully after that. When he finally finished sewing up the man's chest, the attendants in the room cheered. They all congratulated Dr. Cyr for having successfully completed open-heart surgery. They might not have been so happy, however, if they had known the truth. Joseph Cyr was no doctor. He was an impostor—a person pretending to be someone whom he was not. His real name was Ferdinand W. Demara, and not only was he not a doctor, but he had not even finished high school.

Ferdinand Demara was born in Lawrence, Massachusetts, in 1921. He was an extraordinarily bright boy, and schoolwork proved easy for him. In fact, in some ways it was too easy. Demara was bored. He needed something challenging to do, something bold and exciting and important. He believed that he was destined to lead a life of greatness. But there was little opportunity for greatness in the life of a Lawrence schoolboy. By the time Demara was fifteen, he felt he couldn't wait any longer. He had to get out and make his mark in the world. So one morning, instead of going to school, Demara went to the railroad station and hopped a train out of town.

He spent the next several years trying to find the perfect outlet for his talents. He tried doing charity work and teaching at a Catholic boy's school. He even spent some time training to be a monk. But none of those endeavors worked out. Demara kept longing for something more glamorous. It occurred to him that soldiers had plenty of opportunities for glory and excitement. So in 1941, without a second thought, he joined the United States Army. It turned out, though, that a soldier's life was less dramatic than it appeared. Mostly it involved a lot of marching and taking orders and crawling through mud. After just a few weeks, Demara knew that the army would soon be missing one soldier.

To escape, he stole all the identification of a fellow soldier named Anthony Ignolia. He then simply walked off the army base and began life as Anthony Ignolia. Demara used the name for several months. By early 1942, though, he was feeling restless again. He still had visions of having a distinguished military career. Since World War II had broken out, he decided to try once again to serve his country. Under the name Fred W. Demara, he joined the U.S. Navy.

Within several weeks, Demara could see that the navy was just as dull as the army. After considering his options, he decided he might like to be a doctor. The navy's

hospital school wouldn't take him, though, since he didn't even have a high school diploma. Demara fumed at the rejection. He knew how smart he was. In his heart, he knew he would make a brilliant doctor. For that matter, he knew he would make a brilliant military leader or professor or bishop. He simply didn't have the patience to go through the training. He couldn't stand the thought of spending years working his way up a career ladder. What he really wanted was just to wake up one day and *be* somebody important.

When Demara thought of it that way, suddenly it all seemed clear. He would steal the credentials of someone important, and pretend to be that person. That way he could reap the rewards of an exciting profession without going through years of tedious training. Demara searched a college catalog for the name of a faculty member who sounded interesting. He picked a man named Dr. Robert Linton French. French was a professor of psychology who had left teaching to fight in the war. Using personalized stationery with French's name on it, and a post office box address, Demara wrote for copies of French's credentials. Once he had them, he deserted the navy and assumed the identity of Dr. Robert Linton French.

Pretending to be a psychology professor

required more effort than pretending to be Anthony Ignolia. Demara had to display poise, knowledge, and confidence. He succeeded beautifully. For two years he moved from town to town posing as Dr. French. Then, in the fall of 1945, he won a job as a dean at Gannon University in Pennsylvania. That appointment lasted over a year. Demara proved to be a popular teacher. He stayed one step ahead of his students by using every spare minute to read psychology books. Often he became so absorbed in studying that he would be late to class. He would burst into the classroom, look around in bewilderment, and ask, "What am I teaching?" The students thought it was a great joke. They didn't realize their professor was serious.

After a while, though, people began to get suspicious. So Demara sneaked out of town and moved on to new roles. He used stolen credentials to pose as a law student, a cancer researcher, and a zoologist.

Then in 1951 he finally got to be a doctor. He got his hands on the credentials of a surgeon named Joseph Cyr. Pretending to be Cyr, he joined the Royal Canadian Navy. He began performing operations, including the open-heart surgery that brought him such admiration. He completed that surgery on board a navy destroyer in the middle of the Korean combat zone. A storm had blown up, and the ship tossed and pitched furiously. Crew members strung up emergency lights in the commander's cabin. They then watched in awe as Dr. Cyr saved the life of a wounded Korean soldier.

It was one of Demara's finest moments. The Canadian press even ran a story about the doctor's heroic work. Unfortunately for Demara, the article ran in the hometown paper of the real Joseph Cyr. The doctor spoke up, and Demara suddenly found himself in police custody. Canadian officials were terribly embarrassed by the incident. They quickly sent Demara back to the United States.

For several years after that, Demara wandered around the United States under a variety of names. In the mid-1950s he obtained the credentials of a man named B. W. Jones. He went to Texas and used Jones's papers to land a job as a guard in the Huntsville maximum security prison. He made a great impression and was soon promoted to assistant warden. Later he went to the small Maine village of North Haven, pretending to be a teacher named Martin Godgart. There he taught elementary school, became a Sea Scout leader, and played the local Santa Claus at Christmastime.

Eventually the law caught up with Demara. He was arrested in Maine for using a false identity. As usual, though, no one wanted to press charges. Even after learning about all his lies and all his tricks, people still liked Demara. One woman even wanted to marry him. While posing as Dr. Joseph Cyr, Demara had become engaged to a Canadian nurse.

Even after learning that he was a fraud, she wrote him a letter declaring that she still loved him and would happily marry him. She was not the only one who remained loyal to the "Great Impostor." Demara's crew mates from the Royal Canadian Navy still sent him an occasional Christmas card. The prison warden in Texas always spoke fondly of him. And the people of North Haven formed a committee for his defense.

Demara had several more adventures in his wild career as an impostor. He showed up in Mexico as an architect on a bridge construction project. He spent time in Alaska as a teacher at an Eskimo school. He even went to Cuba in hopes of running a prison there. In the end, though, Demara grew tired of his false, unsettled life. He gave up all his disguises and settled down in California under his real name. He spent his last years there, working as a counselor at a local hospital. ∎

If you have been timed while reading this selection, enter your reading time below. Then turn to the Words per Minute table on page 155 and look up your reading speed (words per minute). Enter your reading speed on the graph on page 156.

READING TIME: Unit 19

_____ : _____
Minutes   *Seconds*

How well did you read?

- *Answer the four types of questions that follow. The directions for each type of question tell you how to mark your answers.*

- *When you have finished all four exercises, check your work by using the answer key on page 152. For each right answer, put a check mark (✔) on the line beside the box. For each wrong answer, write the correct answer on the line.*

- *For scoring each exercise, follow the directions below the questions.*

A FINDING THE MAIN IDEA

Look at the three statements below. One expresses the main idea of the story you just read. A good main idea statement answers two questions: it tells *who* or *what* is the subject of the story, and it answers the understood question *does what?* or *is what?* Another statement is *too broad*, it is vague and doesn't tell much about the topic of the story. The third statement is *too narrow*, it tells about only one part of the story.

Match the statements with the three answer choices below by writing the letter of each answer in the box in front of the statement it goes with.

M—Main Idea   **B—Too Broad**   **N—Too Narrow**

____ ☐ 1. Ferdinand Demara was a brilliant impostor who successfully posed as a variety of professional people in highly responsible positions.

____ ☐ 2. Ferdinand Demara was a very bright man whose desire for instant prestige led him to do all sorts of outrageous things.

____ ☐ 3. Ferdinand Demara posed as a surgeon and successfully performed open-heart surgery.

____ Score 15 points for a correct *M* answer
____ Score 5 points for each correct *B* or *N* answer
____ TOTAL SCORE: Finding the Main Idea

B RECALLING FACTS

How well do you remember the facts in the story you just read? Put an *x* in the box in front of the correct answer to each of the multiple choice questions below.

1. Demara joined the United States Army because he
    - ____ ☐ a. was looking for glory and excitement.
    - ____ ☐ b. wanted to fight in Korea.
    - ____ ☐ c. enjoyed marching and drilling.

2. The navy's hospital school would not admit Demara because he
    - ____ ☐ a. had deserted the army.
    - ____ ☐ b. wasn't qualified.
    - ____ ☐ c. didn't have enough money to pay the tuition.

3. Demara saved the life of a wounded Korean soldier by
    - ____ ☐ a. bringing him to the home of Dr. Joseph Cyr.
    - ____ ☐ b. carrying him off the battlefield.
    - ____ ☐ c. performing open-heart surgery on him.

4. While posing as B.W. Jones in Texas, Demara
    - ____ ☐ a. fell in love with a nurse.
    - ____ ☐ b. became assistant warden of a prison.
    - ____ ☐ c. became an elementary school teacher.

5. When Demara was arrested in North Haven, Maine, the local citizens
    - ____ ☐ a. threatened to kill him.
    - ____ ☐ b. filed a suit against him.
    - ____ ☐ c. formed a committee for his defense.

Score 5 points for each correct answer

____ TOTAL SCORE: Recalling Facts

C MAKING INFERENCES

An inference is a judgment that is made or an idea that is arrived at based on facts or on information that is given. You make an inference when you understand something that is *not* stated directly, but that is *implied,* or suggested by the facts that are given.

Below are five statements that are judgments or ideas that have been arrived at from the facts of the story. Write the letter *C* in the box in front of each statement that is a correct inference. Write the letter *F* in front of each faulty inference.

C—Correct Inference   **F—Faulty Inference**

- ____ ☐ 1. Demara's hometown of Lawrence, Massachusetts, was not a very exciting place in the 1920s and 1930s.
- ____ ☐ 2. Ferdinand Demara was an unfriendly person.
- ____ ☐ 3. Ferdinand Demara was a hard worker.
- ____ ☐ 4. Demara enjoyed physical work best.
- ____ ☐ 5. Demara's fiancée did not care what Demara's true identity was.

Score 5 points for each correct answer

____ TOTAL SCORE: Making Inferences

D USING WORDS PRECISELY

Each of the numbered sentences below contains an underlined word or phrase from the story you have just read. Under the sentence are three definitions. One has the *same* meaning as the underlined word or phrase, one has *almost the same* meaning, and one has the *opposite* meaning. Match the definitions with the three answer choices by writing the letter that stands for each answer in the box in front of the definition it goes with.

S—Same   A—Almost the Same   O—Opposite

1. He believed that he was <u>destined</u> to lead a life of greatness.

____ ☐ a. bound by fate

____ ☐ b. denied the right

____ ☐ c. inclined toward

2. He spent the next several years trying to find the perfect <u>outlet</u> for his talents.

____ ☐ a. activity

____ ☐ b. channel of expression

____ ☐ c. trap

3. He still had visions of having a <u>distinguished</u> military career.

____ ☐ a. inferior

____ ☐ b. fine

____ ☐ c. outstanding

4. That way he could reap the rewards of an exciting profession without going through the years of <u>tedious</u> training.

____ ☐ a. tiring

____ ☐ b. boring

____ ☐ c. interesting

5. They then watched in <u>awe</u> as Dr. Cyr saved the life of a wounded Korean soldier.

____ ☐ a. surprise

____ ☐ b. calm acceptance

____ ☐ c. amazement

____ Score 3 points for each correct *S* answer
____ Score 1 point for each correct *A* or *O* answer

____ **TOTAL SCORE:** Using Words Precisely

● *Enter the four total scores in the spaces below, and add them together to find your Critical Reading Score. Then record your Critical Reading Score on the graph on page 157.*

_____	Finding the Main Idea
_____	Recalling Facts
_____	Making Inferences
_____	Using Words Precisely
_____	**CRITICAL READING SCORE: Unit 19**

Would you trust your health to the man in this picture? Many people did, for Dr. William Price was a respected physician. It so happened that he also believed that he was a high priest of a group of prophets and magicians who everyone else thought had died out about 1,800 years before. He practiced ancient rituals that included loud, late-night noises and occasional jaunts around the countryside with nothing on. Though many people were aghast at his strange ideas and behavior, he won a large number of loyal disciples.

William Price: The Last of the Druids

It began as a strange howling noise in the middle of the night. Before long, everyone in the town of Pontypridd, Wales, had been awakened by it. No one knew what the sound was, but people could tell that it was coming from the center of town. One by one, the frightened citizens crawled from their beds and headed toward the town square. Once there, they simply stood and stared in disbelief. William Price, their local doctor, was carrying on wildly in the middle of the common. He wore a bright red and green suit, and a fox skin covered his head. The fox's head rested on Dr. Price's, and its legs dangled around his face. Dr. Price paid no attention to the astonished townspeople. He was too busy dancing around and howling at the moon.

It turned out that Dr. Price was performing a Druid ritual. The Druids were an ancient order of Irish and Welsh priests and prophets. About two thousand years ago, Druids were the leaders of their tribal communities. They served as religious leaders, medicine men, and fortune-tellers. They were also historians, preserving the story of their people through songs and poems, which they wrote in their own special alphabet. Most people thought the Druids had been wiped out in A.D. 43, when the Romans invaded Wales. But

William Price, who was born in 1800, meant to prove that the Druid culture was still alive.

The people of Pontypridd were stunned. They knew that Dr. Price spent much of his spare time studying the ancient symbols and legends of the Druids, but they had assumed it was just a hobby. They thought of Price as a skilled doctor and brilliant surgeon. He had once amazed even his fellow physicians by successfully grafting a bone from a calf's leg into the crushed leg of a coal miner. The townspeople had always felt lucky to have such a respected professional in their midst. Still, they had always known there was something a bit strange about William Price.

Even as a young boy, Price had exhibited certain eccentricities. He ate only fruits and vegetables, and he drank nothing but cider and champagne. He carried a large walking stick whose top was shaped like a crescent moon. He usually dressed in scarlet pants and a bright green jacket. Sometimes, though, he shocked his neighbors by wandering the countryside naked.

On the night that the townsfolk saw him wearing the fox skin and howling at the moon, they realized that his interest in Druid culture was more than a hobby. It

was an obsession. Price had concluded that he was a direct descendant of the Druids. He had gone to the Pontypridd town square to declare himself Archdruid, or head of the Druids.

Like earlier Druids, William Price worshipped nature. Baying at the moon was one way of paying homage to nature. He also honored it by taking an occasional walk in the nude. He knew such actions angered many people, but he didn't care. He didn't believe in society's rules. He advocated a return to a simpler society— one without human regulations. The only laws he recognized were the laws of nature. He condemned institutions such as marriage and organized religions. He was also against political organizations, businesses, and hospitals.

Soon after proclaiming himself Archdruid, Price went to court to demand that a piece of property that had belonged to Druids eighteen centuries earlier be turned over to him. As proof of his right to the land, he presented a 725-page statement that he himself had written. In the statement, Price proclaimed that as Archdruid he had the right to govern the world. The High Court judge remained unconvinced. He denied Price's claim to the land.

Some people shook their heads in disgust at Price's scandalous actions. But others found him an alluring figure. More and more people turned to him as their physical and spiritual leader.

Although he finally renounced all modern forms of medicine, his medical practice grew steadily. His followers seemed entranced by his mystical healing ceremonies and herbal remedies. For the rest of his life, Price remained a popular physician. He kept a full schedule of patients until a week before his death at age ninety-three.

Price also developed a devoted group of religious followers. His admirers formed a secret society of Druids and elected him their head. At a special torchlight meeting, he announced that the time had come for the Druids to take over the government. He declared that they must "strike with all [their] might and power." He added, "I am with you all the way—I, Dr. William Price!" Four thousand devoted followers took him at his word. They grabbed rifles, muskets, and clubs, and marched into the town of Newport. When the police began fighting them off, however, William Price's actions were somewhat less aggressive than his words. He turned and ran, later escaping to England disguised as a woman. He returned only after the uprising had been thoroughly crushed.

That ill-fated revolt was not the only instance in which Price challenged the law. He became involved in countless lawsuits. He often used his time in court to mock the legal system that he despised. Once, for example, he took his infant daughter into the courtroom and introduced her as his "learned counsel." On another occasion, he tried to recover an old family estate by claiming that his father had been insane when he sold it. To prove his point, Price dug up his father's grave and tried to introduce the old man's skull as evidence. He claimed that its shape showed clear signs of insanity.

Despite his failures in the courts and on the battlefield, Price remained a magnetic figure. Even as an old man, he continued to draw admirers from around the Welsh countryside. He also continued to wear his fox-skin headdress and practice his Druid rituals, complete with dancing, chanting, and an occasional howl at the moon. When he died in January of 1893, his funeral became almost a national event. Twenty thousand mourners turned out to bid him farewell. ■

If you have been timed while reading this selection, enter your reading time below. Then turn to the Words per Minute table on page 155 and look up your reading speed (words per minute). Enter your reading speed on the graph on page 156.

READING TIME: Unit 20

_____ : _____
Minutes   *Seconds*

How well did you read?

- *Answer the four types of questions that follow. The directions for each type of question tell you how to mark your answers.*

- *When you have finished all four exercises, check your work by using the answer key on page 152. For each right answer, put a check mark (✓) on the line beside the box. For each wrong answer, write the correct answer on the line.*

- *For scoring each exercise, follow the directions below the questions.*

A FINDING THE MAIN IDEA

Look at the three statements below. One expresses the main idea of the story you just read. A good main idea statement answers two questions: it tells *who* or *what* is the subject of the story, and it answers the understood question *does what?* or *is what?* Another statement is *too broad,* it is vague and doesn't tell much about the topic of the story. The third statement is *too narrow,* it tells about only one part of the story.

Match the statements with the three answer choices below by writing the letter of each answer in the box in front of the statement it goes with.

M—Main Idea   B—Too Broad   N—Too Narrow

_____ ☐ 1. Druids were an ancient order of priests and prophets who lived in Ireland and Wales about two thousand years ago.

_____ ☐ 2. William Price believed he was a direct descendant of the ancient Druids.

_____ ☐ 3. Hundreds of years after the time of the Druids, some people still tried to preserve the Druid culture.

_____ Score 15 points for a correct *M* answer

_____ Score 5 points for each correct *B* or *N* answer

_____ TOTAL SCORE: Finding the Main Idea

B RECALLING FACTS

How well do you remember the facts in the story you just read? Put an x in the box in front of the correct answer to each of the multiple choice questions below.

1. Most people believed the Druids had been wiped out in A.D. 43 when Wales was invaded by the
   ___ ☐ a. Romans.
   ___ ☐ b. English.
   ___ ☐ c. Greeks.

2. While performing Druid rituals, Price often covered his head with
   ___ ☐ a. feathers.
   ___ ☐ b. a scarlet shawl.
   ___ ☐ c. a fox skin.

3. When Price's followers staged a revolt in Newport, Price
   ___ ☐ a. fled to England.
   ___ ☐ b. took them to court.
   ___ ☐ c. resigned as Archdruid.

4. Price condemned
   ___ ☐ a. modern churches and hospitals.
   ___ ☐ b. herbal remedies.
   ___ ☐ c. all alcoholic beverages.

5. Price's funeral was attended by
   ___ ☐ a. everyone in Wales.
   ___ ☐ b. only his immediate family.
   ___ ☐ c. twenty thousand people.

Score 5 points for each correct answer

___ TOTAL SCORE: Recalling Facts

C MAKING INFERENCES

An inference is a judgment that is made or an idea that is arrived at based on facts or on information that is given. You make an inference when you understand something that is *not* stated directly, but that is *implied*, or suggested by the facts that are given.

Below are five statements that are judgments or ideas that have been arrived at from the facts of the story. Write the letter C in the box in front of each statement that is a correct inference. Write the letter F in front of each faulty inference.

C—Correct Inference   F—Faulty Inference

___ ☐ 1. The ancient Druids sometimes howled at the moon.

___ ☐ 2. Dr. Price was often arrested for breaking the law.

___ ☐ 3. Price condemned the use of all weapons.

___ ☐ 4. Many people lost faith in Dr. Price as a doctor when he declared himself a Druid.

___ ☐ 5. Today there are thousands of Druids living in Wales.

Score 5 points for each correct answer

___ TOTAL SCORE: Making Inferences

D USING WORDS PRECISELY

Each of the numbered sentences below contains an underlined word or phrase from the story you have just read. Under the sentence are three definitions. One has the *same* meaning as the underlined word or phrase, one has *almost the same* meaning, and one has the *opposite* meaning. Match the definitions with the three answer choices by writing the letter that stands for each answer in the box in front of the definition it goes with.

S—Same   A—Almost the Same   O—Opposite

1. Some people shook their heads in disgust at Price's scandalous actions.

____ ☐ a. inappropriate

____ ☐ b. proper

____ ☐ c. disgraceful

2. Baying at the moon was one way of paying homage to nature.

____ ☐ a. tribute

____ ☐ b. disrespect

____ ☐ c. compliments

3. Although he finally renounced all modern forms of medicine, his medical practice grew steadily.

____ ☐ a. rejected

____ ☐ b. condemned

____ ☐ c. adopted

4. His followers seemed entranced by his mystical healing ceremonies and herbal remedies.

____ ☐ a. filled with wonder

____ ☐ b. delighted

____ ☐ c. bored

5. That ill-fated revolt was not the only instance in which Price challenged the law.

____ ☐ a. triumphant

____ ☐ b. unsuccessful

____ ☐ c. unlucky

____ Score 3 points for each correct S answer

____ Score 1 point for each correct A or O answer

____ TOTAL SCORE: Using Words Precisely

● *Enter the four total scores in the spaces below, and add them together to find your Critical Reading Score. Then record your Critical Reading Score on the graph on page 157.*

_____ Finding the Main Idea

_____ Recalling Facts

_____ Making Inferences

_____ Using Words Precisely

_____ CRITICAL READING SCORE: Unit 20

Geoffrey Pyke and the Frozen Battleship

Geoffrey Pyke could hardly contain his enthusiasm. He had just invented something he believed would end World War II. Pyke wanted to build huge pipelines that could be strung from English ships to the shores of enemy territory. He believed that soldiers aboard the vessels could then be enclosed in capsules and pumped through the pipelines. When the soldiers reached the shores, they could spring out of the capsules, surprise the enemy, and quickly achieve victory. The plan, however, never found any supporters.

The idea of pumping men through pipelines was not the first farfetched idea Geoffrey Pyke ever had, nor was it the last. Pyke, who lived from 1894 until 1948, spent his entire life thinking up novel solutions to problems. In 1939, for instance, he hatched a scheme to prevent World War II from ever starting. Pyke sent a group of ten college students into Germany posing as golfers. He instructed them to conduct secret interviews with German citizens to find out their views on the war that was brewing. He believed the poll would show that the German people did not want to go to war. When Hitler saw the results, Pyke thought, he would naturally bow to the will of the people and cancel his war plans. Pyke never got to see how that plan would work either.

Before he could compile the results of the poll, Hitler invaded Poland.

Once the war started, Pyke became a civilian consultant for Britain's military planning office. He reported directly to Lord Louis Mountbatten, a close advisor to Prime Minister Winston Churchill. Pyke took his job very seriously. He worked feverishly, turning out one idea after another. One suggestion he made was that commando attack forces be disguised as fire fighters in order to get past enemy guards. He also created a plan to disguise tanks as portable toilets for German officers. He even suggested that German soldiers could be tricked into surrendering by an English soldier disguised as Hitler. Like his giant pipelines, however, those ideas died without ever being tried.

Still, Pyke kept at it. He had so many ideas that he could barely keep up with them all. He became intolerant of anything that wasted his time. He stopped shaving and no longer bothered to wash or iron his clothes. Eventually he even began doing most of his work in bed because that saved him the trouble of getting dressed. He let papers, empty bottles, and cigarette butts clutter his bedroom. He didn't want to waste time making trips to the trash can. At the peak of his productivity, he designed and built a system for

suspending all his furniture from the ceiling. He hung everything on ropes so that he wouldn't waste steps by having to walk around things. Whenever he needed a desk, a chair, or a reading lamp, he would simply lower it to the floor. When he was finished with it, he would raise it back to the ceiling.

In early 1942, Pyke came up with his greatest idea of all. He designed a ship that would revolutionize warfare. The ship would be bigger than anything else on the sea. It would measure two thousand feet long and three hundred feet wide. It would weigh two million tons and be capable of carrying eighty times as much as regular cargo ships. It would easily accommodate two hundred fighter planes and an additional hundred bombers. It would be relatively cheap to build and would require only a small crew. Best of all, Pyke's amazing vessel would be unsinkable, for the entire ship would be made of ice!

Of course, Pyke did not suggest using ordinary ice for his creation. It could be crushed too easily, and it would melt. No, Pyke had made an amazing discovery. He had found that ice containing 14 percent sawdust had remarkable properties. The material, later named pykrete in honor of its inventor, could withstand high temperatures. A cube of pykrete dropped into hot water just bobbed around, showing no signs of melting. Pykrete also proved to be incredibly strong. A one-inch diameter column of it could support a full-size car. Bullets fired from close range either bounced off or penetrated no more than six and a half inches. Hammers and axes could not dent it. A ship made of pykrete could not be seriously damaged by explosives, fire bombs, or torpedoes. It would be, in short, the perfect warship.

Once Pyke had worked out all the details for a pykrete ship, he sent a 232-page memo to Lord Mountbatten. In it, Pyke explained the concept of a frozen battleship. He also went on to detail many other possible uses for pykrete. He believed that in addition to the main ship smaller ice vessels could be built. The smaller ships could be carried aboard the mother ship and launched from pykrete ramps. The smaller ships could then cruise the seas looking for hostile vessels. Upon spotting one, the little ice ships could use special spray guns to form pykrete bridges to the deck of the enemy ship. Soldiers could then run across the bridges to capture the enemy ship. The soldiers could also use their spray guns to freeze the enemy's weapons.

Pyke went on to suggest that some

Geoffrey Pyke never stopped churning out plans and inventions. Though many were too far-out to be practical, some were touched with genius. The British hired Pyke to help them find a way to win World War II. He dreamed up a magnificent secret weapon: a battleship made of ice.

dummy ice ships—decoys—could be created, as well. The dummies would be ordinary ice—perhaps sawed-off pieces of icebergs. The giant ice cubes would help frighten and confuse the enemy. The Germans might even waste valuable ammunition trying to destroy them. Pyke suggested that some of the dummy ships be equipped with giant neon signs to taunt enemy bomber pilots. The signs would read, "BOMB ME—I'M A DUMMY!"

Finally, Pyke proposed that pykrete could be used to freeze entire cities into submission. He believed that by shooting pykrete from giant spray guns, all entrances to enemy cities could be cut off, trapping the inhabitants inside.

When Lord Mountbatten read Pyke's lengthy memo, he became very excited. He obtained a small block of pykrete from Pyke, then hurried off to see Winston Churchill. Churchill was taking a bath when Mountbatten burst in on him. Mountbatten dropped the pykrete into the prime minister's steaming bath water, then stepped back triumphantly. When Churchill saw that the special ice did not melt, he too became enthusiastic. Calling the new substance "dazzling,"

he wrote a top secret letter to one of his generals. In it he said, "I attach the greatest importance to the prompt examination of [Pyke's] ideas. . . ."

That fall, English scientists used pykrete to build a test ship on a remote lake in Canada. It measured sixty feet in length and weighed a thousand tons. As Pyke had predicted, the ship appeared to be perfect. Throughout the hot summer of 1943, it neither melted nor evaporated. That good news prompted Churchill to meet with Franklin Roosevelt, the president of the United States. Churchill poured scalding water over a cube of pykrete to demonstrate to Roosevelt its marvelous qualities. At the end of the demonstration, Roosevelt agreed that the United States Navy should join England in the development of Pyke's frozen battleship.

Scientists picked a deserted spot in Newfoundland as the construction site. Pyke wanted desperately to be part of the construction team. The Americans, however, refused to work with him. They did not trust a man who looked so shabby, talked so rudely, and had no respect for military regulations. The British, therefore, ordered Pyke to remain in England.

As it turned out, the scientists and construction workers never finished Pyke's giant ice ship. In 1944, the tide of the war turned, and it became clear that Germany would be defeated. After their successful invasion of Normandy in the summer of 1944, the Allies no longer needed a floating ice fortress. And so one of the most imaginative ideas ever conceived was quietly set aside. Geoffrey Pyke's frozen battleship will never be built. The development of nuclear warfare made sure of that. In a modern war, nuclear weapons would turn such a ship into an enormous radioactive blob. ■

If you have been timed while reading this selection, enter your reading time below. Then turn to the Words per Minute table on page 155 and look up your reading speed (words per minute). Enter your reading speed on the graph on page 156.

READING TIME: Unit 21

_____ : _____
Minutes   *Seconds*

How well did you read?

- *Answer the four types of questions that follow. The directions for each type of question tell you how to mark your answers.*

- *When you have finished all four exercises, check your work by using the answer key on page 152. For each right answer, put a check mark (✓) on the line beside the box. For each wrong answer, write the correct answer on the line.*

- *For scoring each exercise, follow the directions below the questions.*

A FINDING THE MAIN IDEA

Look at the three statements below. One expresses the main idea of the story you just read. A good main idea statement answers two questions: it tells *who* or *what* is the subject of the story, and it answers the understood question *does what?* or *is what?* Another statement is *too broad,* it is vague and doesn't tell much about the topic of the story. The third statement is *too narrow,* it tells about only one part of the story.

Match the statements with the three answer choices below by writing the letter of each answer in the box in front of the statement it goes with.

M—Main Idea   **B—Too Broad**   **N—Too Narrow**

____ ☐ 1. Geoffrey Pyke dreamed up many plans and inventions, including his greatest idea—a battleship made of ice.

____ ☐ 2. During World War II, Geoffrey Pyke served as a civilian consultant to Britain's military planning office.

____ ☐ 3. Geoffrey Pyke was a man of unusual imagination and inventiveness.

____ Score 15 points for a correct *M* answer

____ Score 5 points for each correct *B* or *N* answer

____ TOTAL SCORE: Finding the Main Idea

B RECALLING FACTS

How well do you remember the facts in the story you just read? Put an *x* in the box in front of the correct answer to each of the multiple choice questions below.

1. When he worked in the military planning office, Pyke reported directly to
   - ___ ☐ a. Winston Churchill.
   - ___ ☐ b. Louis Mountbatten.
   - ___ ☐ c. Franklin Roosevelt.

2. Pyke believed he could prevent World War II by
   - ___ ☐ a. organizing an international golf tournament.
   - ___ ☐ b. warning Hitler about plans to build pykrete battleships.
   - ___ ☐ c. taking a public opinion poll in Germany and showing it to Hitler.

3. Pykrete was made of
   - ___ ☐ a. wood chips and frozen alcohol.
   - ___ ☐ b. ice and sawdust.
   - ___ ☐ c. sawdust, ice, and neon gas.

4. The pykrete test ship built in the fall of 1943
   - ___ ☐ a. melted in the summer heat.
   - ___ ☐ b. sank in a Canadian lake.
   - ___ ☐ c. neither melted nor evaporated.

5. A pykrete ship would not be a good military weapon today because
   - ___ ☐ a. it would be too expensive to build.
   - ___ ☐ b. it could not withstand the effects of nuclear weapons.
   - ___ ☐ c. it would move too slowly.

Score 5 points for each correct answer

___ TOTAL SCORE: Recalling Facts

C MAKING INFERENCES

An inference is a judgment that is made or an idea that is arrived at based on facts or on information that is given. You make an inference when you understand something that is *not* stated directly, but that is *implied,* or suggested by the facts that are given.

Below are five statements that are judgments or ideas that have been arrived at from the facts of the story. Write the letter *C* in the box in front of each statement that is a correct inference. Write the letter *F* in front of each faulty inference.

C—Correct Inference   F—Faulty Inference

- ___ ☐ 1. Military leaders thought Pyke's ideas were too weird to be taken seriously.
- ___ ☐ 2. A pykrete ship would not be seriously damaged if it hit another ship.
- ___ ☐ 3. The giant pykrete spray guns that Pyke envisioned were never actually built.
- ___ ☐ 4. People found it pleasant to work with Pyke.
- ___ ☐ 5. Pyke was disappointed that his battleship was never built.

Score 5 points for each correct answer

___ TOTAL SCORE: Making Inferences

D USING WORDS PRECISELY

Each of the numbered sentences below contains an underlined word or phrase from the story you have just read. Under the sentence are three definitions. One has the *same* meaning as the underlined word or phrase, one has *almost the same* meaning, and one has the *opposite* meaning. Match the definitions with the three answer choices by writing the letter that stands for each answer in the box in front of the definition it goes with.

S—Same   A—Almost the Same   O—Opposite

1. Pyke, who lived from 1894 until 1948, spent his entire life thinking up <u>novel</u> solutions to problems.

____ ☐ a. ordinary

____ ☐ b. original

____ ☐ c. creative

2. Before he could <u>compile</u> the results of the poll, Hitler invaded Poland.

____ ☐ a. arrange

____ ☐ b. scatter

____ ☐ c. collect and organize

3. He became <u>intolerant</u> of anything that wasted his time.

____ ☐ a. unable to bear

____ ☐ b. accepting

____ ☐ c. impatient

4. It would easily <u>accommodate</u> two hundred fighter planes and an additional hundred bomber planes.

____ ☐ a. have room for

____ ☐ b. exclude

____ ☐ c. arrange

5. Pyke suggested that some of the dummy ships be equipped with giant neon signs to <u>taunt</u> enemy bomber pilots.

____ ☐ a. please

____ ☐ b. tease

____ ☐ c. torment

____ Score 3 points for each correct *S* answer

____ Score 1 point for each correct *A* or *O* answer

____ TOTAL SCORE: Using Words Precisely

● *Enter the four total scores in the spaces below, and add them together to find your Critical Reading Score. Then record your Critical Reading Score on the graph on page 157.*

_____ Finding the Main Idea

_____ Recalling Facts

_____ Making Inferences

_____ Using Words Precisely

_____ CRITICAL READING SCORE: Unit 21

ANSWER KEY

1 Snowflake Bentley
A. Finding the Main Idea
1. **B**   2. **N**   3. **M**

B. Recalling Facts
1. **b**   2. **a**   3. **c**   4. **c**   5. **b**

C. Making Inferences
1. **C**   2. **C**   3. **F**   4. **F**   5. **F**

D. Using Words Precisely
1. a. **S**   b. **O**   c. **A**
2. a. **S**   b. **A**   c. **O**
3. a. **A**   b. **S**   c. **O**
4. a. **O**   b. **A**   c. **S**
5. a. **A**   b. **S**   c. **O**

2 Jay Johnstone: Major League Clown
A. Finding the Main Idea
1. **M**   2. **B**   3. **N**

B. Recalling Facts
1. **a**   2. **b**   3. **b**   4. **c**   5. **a**

C. Making Inferences
1. **C**   2. **F**   3. **C**   4. **F**   5. **F**

D. Using Words Precisely
1. a. **O**   b. **S**   c. **A**
2. a. **S**   b. **A**   c. **O**
3. a. **O**   b. **S**   c. **A**
4. a. **S**   b. **O**   c. **A**
5. a. **O**   b. **A**   c. **S**

3 Black Bart: Gentle Bandit
A. Finding the Main Idea
1. **N**   2. **M**   3. **B**

B. Recalling Facts
1. **b**   2. **c**   3. **b**   4. **a**   5. **b**

C. Making Inferences
1. **C**   2. **C**   3. **F**   4. **F**   5. **C**

D. Using Words Precisely
1. a. **O**   b. **S**   c. **A**
2. a. **S**   b. **O**   c. **A**
3. a. **O**   b. **S**   c. **A**
4. a. **O**   b. **A**   c. **S**
5. a. **S**   b. **A**   c. **O**

4 George Kaufman: Keeping Fit
A. Finding the Main Idea
1. **N**   2. **M**   3. **B**

B. Recalling Facts
1. **b**   2. **b**   3. **a**   4. **c**   5. **c**

C. Making Inferences
1. **F**   2. **F**   3. **C**   4. **F**   5. **C**

D. Using Words Precisely
1. a. **S**   b. **O**   c. **A**
2. a. **O**   b. **A**   c. **S**
3. a. **A**   b. **S**   c. **O**
4. a. **O**   b. **S**   c. **A**
5. a. **S**   b. **O**   c. **A**

5 Johnny Appleseed
A. Finding the Main Idea
1. **N**   2. **B**   3. **M**

B. Recalling Facts
1. **a**   2. **c**   3. **b**   4. **a**   5. **a**

C. Making Inferences
1. **F**   2. **F**   3. **C**   4. **F**   5. **C**

D. Using Words Precisely
1. a. **O**   b. **A**   c. **S**
2. a. **S**   b. **A**   c. **O**
3. a. **A**   b. **S**   c. **O**
4. a. **S**   b. **A**   c. **O**
5. a. **A**   b. **S**   c. **O**

6 Diamond Jim Brady
A. Finding the Main Idea
1. **M**   2. **N**   3. **B**

B. Recalling Facts
1. **b**   2. **c**   3. **a**   4. **a**   5. **b**

C. Making Inferences
1. **F**   2. **F**   3. **C**   4. **C**   5. **F**

D. Using Words Precisely
1. a. **O**   b. **S**   c. **A**
2. a. **A**   b. **O**   c. **S**
3. a. **A**   b. **S**   c. **O**
4. a. **S**   b. **O**   c. **A**
5. a. **S**   b. **A**   c. **O**

7 Sylvester Graham: You Are What You Eat
A. Finding the Main Idea
1. **M**   2. **N**   3. **B**

B. Recalling Facts
1. **b**   2. **c**   3. **c**   4. **b**   5. **a**

C. Making Inferences
1. **C**   2. **F**   3. **F**   4. **F**   5. **C**

D. Using Words Precisely
1. a. **A**   b. **O**   c. **S**
2. a. **S**   b. **O**   c. **A**
3. a. **A**   b. **S**   c. **O**
4. a. **O**   b. **S**   c. **A**
5. a. **S**   b. **A**   c. **O**

8 Hugh Troy: Just Joking

A. Finding the Main Idea
   1. N   2. B   3. M

B. Recalling Facts
   1. b   2. c   3. b   4. b   5. a

C. Making Inferences
   1. C   2. C   3. F   4. C   5. F

D. Using Words Precisely
   1. a. O b. A c. S
   2. a. S b. O c. A
   3. a. A b. S c. O
   4. a. A b. O c. S
   5. a. S b. A c. O

9 John Cleves Symmes and the Hollow Earth

A. Finding the Main Idea
   1. N   2. B   3. M

B. Recalling Facts
   1. b   2. b   3. a   4. c   5. b

C. Making Inferences
   1. F   2. C   3. F   4. C   5. F

D. Using Words Precisely
   1. a. O b. S c. A
   2. a. O b. S c. A
   3. a. S b. A c. O
   4. a. S b. A c. O
   5. a. S b. O c. A

10 Hetty Green: Money Was Everything

A. Finding the Main Idea
   1. M   2. N   3. B

B. Recalling Facts
   1. b   2. b   3. a   4. b   5. c

C. Making Inferences
   1. F   2. F   3. C   4. F   5. F

D. Using Words Precisely
   1. a. O b. S c. A
   2. a. S b. A c. O
   3. a. O b. A c. S
   4. a. A b. S c. O
   5. a. S b. A c. O

11 Timothy Dexter's Quest for Renown

A. Finding the Main Idea
   1. M   2. B   3. N

B. Recalling Facts
   1. b   2. c   3. b   4. c   5. a

C. Making Inferences
   1. C   2. C   3. C   4. F   5. F

D. Using Words Precisely
   1. a. S b. O c. A
   2. a. O b. S c. A
   3. a. S b. O c. A
   4. a. O b. S c. A
   5. a. O b. A c. S

12 Bill Veeck: Entertaining the Fans

A. Finding the Main Idea
   1. B   2. M   3. N

B. Recalling Facts
   1. a   2. b   3. c   4. b   5. c

C. Making Inferences
   1. C   2. F   3. C   4. C   5. F

D. Using Words Precisely
   1. a. O b. S c. A
   2. a. S b. A c. O
   3. a. S b. A c. O
   4. a. O b. S c. A
   5. a. A b. S c. O

13 The Dream King

A. Finding the Main Idea
   1. B   2. M   3. N

B. Recalling Facts
   1. c   2. b   3. a   4. c   5. b

C. Making Inferences
   1. C   2. F   3. F   4. F   5. F

D. Using Words Precisely
   1. a. A b. O c. S
   2. a. S b. O c. A
   3. a. S b. A c. O
   4. a. S b. O c. A
   5. a. O b. A c. S

14 Salvador Dali: A Question of Reality

A. Finding the Main Idea
   1. M   2. B   3. N

B. Recalling Facts
   1. c   2. a   3. a   4. c   5. c

C. Making Inferences
   1. F   2. F   3. C   4. F   5. C

D. Using Words Precisely
   1. a. S b. O c. A
   2. a. S b. A c. O
   3. a. O b. S c. A
   4. a. S b. O c. A
   5. a. O b. A c. S

15 Norton I, Emperor of the United States

A. Finding the Main Idea
   1. **M**   2. **N**   3. **B**

B. Recalling Facts
   1. **a**   2. **b**   3. **b**   4. **a**   5. **c**

C. Making Inferences
   1. **F**   2. **C**   3. **C**   4. **C**   5. **F**

D. Using Words Precisely
   1. a. **O**   b. **A**   c. **S**
   2. a. **S**   b. **O**   c. **A**
   3. a. **A**   b. **O**   c. **S**
   4. a. **A**   b. **S**   c. **O**
   5. a. **A**   b. **S**   c. **O**

16 Charles Johnson and the Flat Earth Society

A. Finding the Main Idea
   1. **M**   2. **B**   3. **N**

B. Recalling Facts
   1. **a**   2. **b**   3. **b**   4. **a**   5. **c**

C. Making Inferences
   1. **C**   2. **C**   3. **F**   4. **C**   5. **F**

D. Using Words Precisely
   1. a. **O**   b. **S**   c. **A**
   2. a. **A**   b. **O**   c. **S**
   3. a. **S**   b. **O**   c. **A**
   4. a. **A**   b. **S**   c. **O**
   5. a. **A**   b. **S**   c. **O**

17 Carry Nation: Fighting the "Hellish Poison"

A. Finding the Main Idea
   1. **M**   2. **B**   3. **N**

B. Recalling Facts
   1. **a**   2. **b**   3. **c**   4. **b**   5. **b**

C. Making Inferences
   1. **F**   2. **F**   3. **C**   4. **F**   5. **C**

D. Using Words Precisely
   1. a. **O**   b. **S**   c. **A**
   2. a. **O**   b. **S**   c. **A**
   3. a. **S**   b. **O**   c. **A**
   4. a. **S**   b. **A**   c. **O**
   5. a. **O**   b. **A**   c. **S**

18 Charles Waterton Loved Animals

A. Finding the Main Idea
   1. **N**   2. **M**   3. **B**

B. Recalling Facts
   1. **a**   2. **c**   3. **c**   4. **c**   5. **b**

C. Making Inferences
   1. **F**   2. **C**   3. **F**   4. **F**   5. **C**

D. Using Words Precisely
   1. a. **O**   b. **S**   c. **A**
   2. a. **S**   b. **A**   c. **O**
   3. a. **O**   b. **S**   c. **A**
   4. a. **O**   b. **A**   c. **S**
   5. a. **A**   b. **S**   c. **O**

19 The Great Impostor

A. Finding the Main Idea
   1. **M**   2. **B**   3. **N**

B. Recalling Facts
   1. **a**   2. **b**   3. **c**   4. **b**   5. **c**

C. Making Inferences
   1. **C**   2. **F**   3. **C**   4. **F**   5. **C**

D. Using Words Precisely
   1. a. **S**   b. **O**   c. **A**
   2. a. **A**   b. **S**   c. **O**
   3. a. **O**   b. **A**   c. **S**
   4. a. **A**   b. **S**   c. **O**
   5. a. **A**   b. **O**   c. **S**

20 William Price: The Last of the Druids

A. Finding the Main Idea
   1. **N**   2. **M**   3. **B**

B. Recalling Facts
   1. **a**   2. **c**   3. **a**   4. **a**   5. **c**

C. Making Inferences
   1. **C**   2. **F**   3. **F**   4. **C**   5. **F**

D. Using Words Precisely
   1. a. **A**   b. **O**   c. **S**
   2. a. **S**   b. **O**   c. **A**
   3. a. **S**   b. **A**   c. **O**
   4. a. **S**   b. **A**   c. **O**
   5. a. **O**   b. **S**   c. **A**

21 Geoffrey Pyke and the Frozen Battleship

A. Finding the Main Idea
   1. **M**   2. **N**   3. **B**

B. Recalling Facts
   1. **b**   2. **c**   3. **b**   4. **c**   5. **b**

C. Making Inferences
   1. **F**   2. **C**   3. **C**   4. **F**   5. **C**

D. Using Words Precisely
   1. a. **O**   b. **S**   c. **A**
   2. a. **A**   b. **O**   c. **S**
   3. a. **S**   b. **O**   c. **A**
   4. a. **S**   b. **O**   c. **A**
   5. a. **O**   b. **S**   c. **A**

WORDS PER MINUTE TABLE
& PROGRESS GRAPHS

Second

Words per Minute

Unit ▶	Sample	1	2	3	4	5	6	7	
No. of Words ▶	926	833	940	1092	817	986	1112	933	
1:30	617	555	627	728	545	657	741	622	90
1:40	556	500	564	655	490	592	667	560	100
1:50	505	454	513	596	446	538	607	509	110
2:00	463	417	470	546	409	493	556	467	120
2:10	427	384	434	504	377	455	513	431	130
2:20	397	357	403	468	350	423	477	400	140
2:30	370	333	376	437	327	394	445	373	150
2:40	347	312	353	410	306	370	417	350	160
2:50	327	294	332	385	288	348	392	329	170
3:00	309	278	313	364	272	329	371	311	180
3:10	292	263	297	345	258	311	351	295	190
3:20	278	250	282	328	245	296	334	280	200
3:30	265	238	269	314	233	282	318	267	210
3:40	253	227	256	298	223	269	303	254	220
3:50	242	217	245	285	213	257	290	243	230
4:00	232	208	235	273	204	247	278	233	240
4:10	222	200	226	262	196	237	267	224	250
4:20	214	192	217	252	189	228	257	215	260
4:30	206	185	209	243	182	219	247	207	270
4:40	198	179	201	234	175	211	238	200	280
4:50	192	172	194	226	169	204	230	193	290
5:00	185	167	188	218	163	197	222	187	300
5:10	179	161	182	211	158	191	215	181	310
5:20	174	156	176	205	153	185	208	175	320
5:30	168	151	171	199	149	179	202	170	330
5:40	163	147	166	193	144	174	196	165	340
5:50	159	143	161	187	140	169	191	160	350
6:00	154	139	157	182	136	164	185	156	360
6:10	150	135	152	177	132	160	180	151	370
6:20	146	132	148	172	129	156	176	147	380
6:30	142	128	145	168	126	152	171	144	390
6:40	139	125	141	164	123	148	167	140	400
6:50	136	122	138	160	120	144	163	137	410
7:00	132	119	134	156	117	141	159	133	420
7:20	126	114	128	149	111	134	152	127	440
7:40	121	109	123	142	107	129	145	122	460
8:00	116	104	118	137	102	123	139	117	480

Minutes and Seconds ▶

◀ *Seconds*

GROUP TWO

Unit ▶	8	9	10	11	12	13	14	Seconds ▶
No. of Words ▶	1211	1166	1213	1254	1148	849	1172	
1:30	807	777	809	836	765	566	781	90
1:40	727	700	728	752	689	509	703	100
1:50	661	636	662	684	626	463	639	110
2:00	606	583	607	627	574	425	586	120
2:10	559	538	560	579	530	392	541	130
2:20	519	500	520	537	492	364	502	140
2:30	484	466	485	502	459	340	469	150
2:40	454	437	455	470	431	318	440	160
2:50	427	412	428	443	405	300	414	170
3:00	404	389	404	418	383	280	391	180
3:10	382	368	383	396	363	268	370	190
3:20	363	350	364	376	344	255	352	200
3:30	346	333	347	358	328	243	335	210
3:40	330	318	331	342	313	232	220	220
3:50	316	304	316	327	299	221	306	230
4:00	303	292	303	314	287	212	293	240
4:10	291	280	291	301	276	204	281	250
4:20	279	269	280	289	265	196	270	260
4:30	269	259	270	279	255	189	260	270
4:40	260	250	260	269	246	182	251	280
4:50	251	241	251	259	238	176	242	290
5:00	242	233	243	251	230	170	234	300
5:10	234	226	235	243	222	164	227	310
5:20	227	219	227	235	215	159	220	320
5:30	220	212	221	228	209	154	213	330
5:40	214	206	214	221	203	150	207	340
5:50	208	200	208	215	197	146	201	350
6:00	202	194	202	209	191	142	196	360
6:10	196	189	197	203	186	138	190	370
6:20	191	184	192	198	181	134	185	380
6:30	186	179	187	193	177	131	180	390
6:40	182	175	182	188	172	127	176	400
6:50	177	171	178	184	168	124	172	410
7:00	173	167	173	179	164	121	167	420
7:20	165	159	165	171	157	116	160	440
7:40	158	152	158	164	150	111	153	460
8:00	151	146	152	157	144	106	147	480

Minutes and Seconds (left) / *Seconds* (right)

GROUP THREE

Unit ▶	15	16	17	18	19	20	21	Seconds ▶
No. of Words ▶	1456	1011	1110	1068	1339	1027	1348	
1:30	971	674	740	712	893	685	899	90
1:40	874	607	666	641	803	616	809	100
1:50	794	552	605	583	730	560	735	110
2:00	728	506	555	534	670	514	674	120
2:10	672	467	512	493	618	474	622	130
2:20	624	433	476	458	574	440	578	140
2:30	582	404	444	427	536	411	539	150
2:40	546	379	416	401	502	385	506	160
2:50	514	357	392	377	473	362	476	170
3:00	485	337	370	356	446	342	449	180
3:10	460	319	350	337	423	324	426	190
3:20	437	303	333	320	402	308	404	200
3:30	416	289	317	305	383	293	385	210
3:40	397	276	303	291	365	280	368	220
3:50	380	264	290	279	349	268	352	230
4:00	364	253	278	267	335	257	337	240
4:10	349	243	266	256	321	246	324	250
4:20	336	233	256	246	309	237	311	260
4:30	324	225	247	237	298	228	300	270
4:40	312	217	238	229	287	220	289	280
4:50	301	209	230	221	277	212	279	290
5:00	291	202	222	214	268	205	270	300
5:10	282	196	215	207	259	199	261	310
5:20	273	190	208	200	251	192	253	320
5:30	265	184	202	199	243	187	245	330
5:40	257	178	196	188	236	181	238	340
5:50	250	173	190	183	230	176	231	350
6:00	243	169	185	178	223	171	225	360
6:10	236	164	180	173	217	167	219	370
6:20	230	160	175	169	211	162	213	380
6:30	224	156	171	164	206	158	207	390
6:40	218	152	167	160	201	154	202	400
6:50	213	148	162	156	196	150	197	410
7:00	208	145	159	152	191	147	193	420
7:20	198	138	151	146	185	140	184	440
7:40	190	132	145	139	175	134	176	460
8:00	182	126	139	134	167	128	169	480

Minutes and Seconds (left) / *Seconds* (right)

Reading Speed

Directions: *Write your Words per Minute score for each unit in the box under the number of the unit. Then plot your reading speed on the graph by putting a small* x *on the line directly above the number of the unit, across from the number of words per minute you read. As you mark your speed for each unit, graph your progress by drawing a line to connect the* x's.

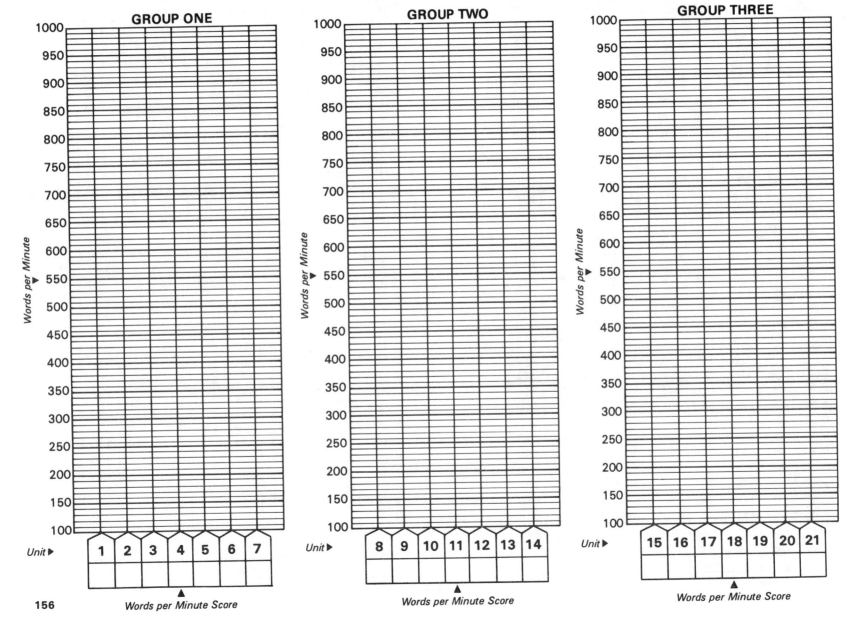

GROUP ONE

GROUP TWO

GROUP THREE

Words per Minute

Words per Minute Score

156

Critical Reading Scores

Directions: *Write your Critical Reading Score for each unit in the box under the number of the unit. Then plot your score on the graph by putting a small **x** on the line directly above the number of the unit, across from the score you earned. As you mark your score for each unit, graph your progress by drawing a line to connect the **x**'s.*

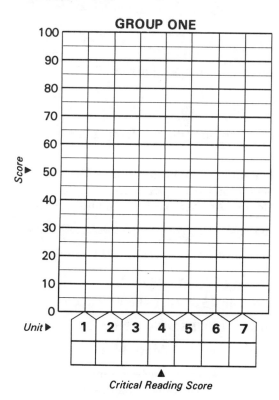

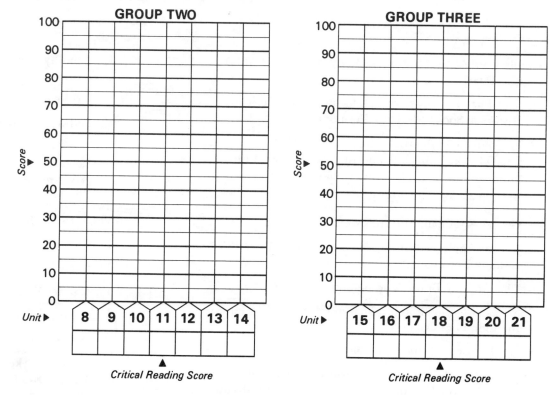

Picture Credits

Sample Unit: Alvin "Shipwreck" Kelly: AP/WIDE WORLD PHOTOS

1. Snowflake Bentley portrait and snowflakes: Jericho Historical Society, Jericho, Vermont

2. Jay Johnstone: Reprinted from TEMPORARY INSANITY, ©1985 by Jay Johnstone and Rick Talley, used with permission of Contemporary Books, Inc., Chicago

3. Black Bart: AP/WIDE WORLD PHOTOS

4. George Kaufman: AP/WIDE WORLD PHOTOS

5. Johnny Appleseed: from *Man and Myth,* by Robert Price, Indiana University Press

6. Diamond Jim Brady: The Bettmann Archive

7. Sylvester Graham: Reproduction from the collections of the Library of Congress

8. Hugh Troy: UPI/Bettmann Newsphotos

9. John Cleves Symmes: Ohio Historical Society. Photo of Earth: National Aeronautics and Space Administration

10. Hetty Green: AP/WIDE WORLD PHOTOS

11. Timothy Dexter: Courtesy of the Newburyport Public Library

12. Bill Veeck, Eddie Gaedel: AP/WIDE WORLD PHOTOS

13. Ludwig II of Bavaria: Rainbird/Robert Harding Picture Library

14. Salvador Dali: The Bettmann Archive. Painting *The Persistence of Memory* (oil on canvas, 9½" x 13"): Collection, The Museum of Modern Art, New York, given anonymously

15. Norton I: California State Library

16. Charles and Marjory Johnson: AP/WIDE WORLD PHOTOS

17. Carry Nation: Brown Brothers, Sterling, PA

18. Charles Waterton: National Portrait Gallery, London

19. Ferdinand W. Demara: AP/WIDE WORLD PHOTOS

20. William Price: Pontypridd Public Library, Wales

21. Geoffrey Pyke: from *Pyke the Unknown Genius,* by David Lampe, Evans Brothers, Ltd. Drawing of battleship: The Illustrated London News Picture Library